Arthur S. Link
Princeton University
General Editor for History

The American History Series
under the series editorship of
John Hope Franklin, *University of Chicago
and National Humanities Center*
Abraham S. Eisenstadt, *Brooklyn College*

Altschuler, Glenn C. • *Race, Ethnicity, and Class in American Social Thought, 1865–1919*

Bartlett, Irving H. • *The American Mind in the Mid-Nineteenth Century,* 2d ed.

Beisner, Robert L. • *From the Old Diplomacy to the New, 1865–1900*

Borden, Morton • *Parties and Politics in the Early Republic, 1789–1815*

Carter, Paul A. • *The Twenties in America,* 2d ed.

Conkin, Paul K. • *The New Deal,* 2d ed.

Dubofsky, Melvyn • *Industrialism and the American Worker, 1865–1920*

Griffin, C. S. • *The Ferment of Reform, 1830–1860*

Kraut, Alan M. • *The Huddled Masses: The Immigrant in American Society, 1880–1921*

Levering, Ralph B. • *The Cold War, 1945–1972*

Martin, James Kirby, and Mark Edward Lender • *A Respectable Army: The Military Origins of the Republic, 1763-1789*

Newmyer, R. Kent • *The Supreme Court Under Marshall and Taney*

Porter, Glenn • *The Rise of Big Business, 1860–1910*

Ubbelohde, Carl • *The American Colonies and the British Empire, 1607–1763,* 2d ed.

Wiltz, John E. • *From Isolation to War, 1931–1941*

Wood, Forrest G. • *The Era of Reconstruction, 1863–1877*

Forthcoming Titles

Flint, Barbara J. • *Black Americans in the Industrial Age, 1865–1920*

Graymont, Barbara • *Red Men and White Men in the Colonial Age*

Harris, William H. • *Black Americans in the Modern Age, 1920–1980*

Link, Arthur S., and Richard L. McCormick • *The Progressive Era*

Mohl, Raymond A. • *Urban Life in the Industrial Age, 1860–1920*

Rabinowitz, Howard N. • *The New South, 1877–1913*

Remini, Robert V. • *The Jacksonian Era*

Cover illustration: Carnegie Library of Pittsburgh

Glenn Porter
HARVARD UNIVERSITY

The Rise of Big Business, 1860-1910

Harlan Davidson, Inc.
Arlington Heights, Illinois 60004

ISBN: 0-88295-750-3
(Formerly 0-690-70394-5)

Library of Congress Card Number: 73-632

For KT, my southern hothouse flower

PRINTED IN THE UNITED STATES OF AMERICA

81 82 83 84 85MA12 11 10 9 8 7

EDITORS' FOREWORD

Every generation writes its own history, for the reason that it sees the past in the foreshortened perspective of its own experience. This has certainly been true of the writing of American history. The practical aim of our historiography is to offer us a more certain sense of where we are going by helping us understand the road we took in getting where we are. If the substance and nature of our historical writing is changing, it is precisely because our own generation is redefining its direction, much as the generations that preceded us redefined theirs. We are seeking a newer direction, because we are facing new problems, changing our values and premises, and shaping new institutions to meet new needs. Thus, the vitality of the present inspires the vitality of our writing about our past. Today's scholars are hard at work reconsidering every major field of our history: its politics, diplomacy, economy, society, mores, values, sexuality, and status, ethnic, and race relations. No less significantly, our scholars are using newer modes of investigation to probe the ever-expanding domain of the American past.

Our aim, in this American History Series, is to offer the reader a survey of what scholars are saying about the central themes and issues of American history. To present these themes and issues, we have invited scholars who have made notable contributions to the respective fields in which they are writing. Each volume offers the reader a sufficient factual and narrative account for perceiving the larger dimensions of its particular subject. Addressing their respective themes, our authors have undertaken, moreover, to present the conclusions derived by the principal writers on these themes. Beyond that, the authors present their own conclusions about those aspects of their respective subjects that have been matters of difference and controversy. In effect, they have written not only about where the subject stands in today's historiography but also about where they stand on their subject. Each volume closes with an extensive critical essay on the writings of the major authorities on its particular theme.

The books in this series are designed for use in both basic and advanced courses in American history. Such a series has a particular utility in times such as these, when the traditional format of our American history courses is being altered to accommodate a greater diversity of texts and reading materials. The series offers a number of distinct advantages. It extends and deepens the dimensions of course work in American history. In proceeding beyond the confines of the traditional textbook, it makes clear that the study of our past is, more than the student might otherwise infer, at once complex, sophisticated, and profound. It presents American history as a subject of continuing vitality and fresh investigation. The work of experts in their respective fields, it opens up to the student the rich findings of historical inquiry. It invites the student to join, in major fields of research, the many groups of scholars who are pondering anew the central themes and problems of our past. It challenges the student to participate actively in exploring American history and to collaborate in the creative and rigorous adventure of seeking out its wider reaches.

John Hope Franklin

Abraham S. Eisenstadt

CONTENTS

ONE

What Is
Big Business?

The purpose of this volume is to impart some information and some ideas about one of the most important, yet widely misunderstood, topics in American history—the coming of big business. The average American has a limited understanding of his society, his government, and his past, but above all, of the economy. This is not entirely his fault. Anyone who has watched economists trade jargon and conflicting predictions may feel that he has fallen among soothsayers just back from examining entrails. As for the public's attitude toward big business, most Americans of the last quarter-century seem to have accepted its existence as a normal and natural part of their lives, like the certainty of taxes and the four seasons. Many citizens, of course, continue to be deeply concerned about abuses of power by large corporations and about the dangers posed by the often intimate connections between business and government. Nevertheless, it is clear that the American political process has accepted the fact of the existence of big business, that large-scale enterprises are not likely to be destroyed or fundamentally altered via political action, though their behavior will continue to be constrained and influenced by political and social criticisms.

Throughout our national history, Americans have shaped much of their politics around one or another variant of the struggle against big business. The lineage of ideas about the evils of large-scale business goes back at least as far as Thomas Jefferson. Andrew Jackson and his followers later molded an era around the fight to destroy the "monster" Bank of the United States and its influence. Both the populist and progressive movements, though extremely complex experiences, were ultimately rooted in a deep reluctance to accept the rise of big business without protest. After an apparent national accommodation with the new economic order in the 1920s, the New Deal witnessed what may well have been the Indian summer of any genuine widespread concern with antitrust movements. The recent rekindling of public interest in the shortcomings of big business, sparked by critics such as Ralph Nader, may develop into a significant political force, though that remains to be seen.

Most of our earlier political conflicts about business, like other political clashes, were couched in very vague terms. Few people were specific about what they meant by big business or how to correct its alleged evils. In addition, the opposition to large-scale business often was mixed with a confused array of related but distinct ideas such as the persistent idealization of rural, agrarian civilization and the rejection of urban, industrial life—what Richard Hofstadter (in *The Age of Reform* [1955]) called the "agrarian myth." Most Americans witnessed in confusion and doubt the passing of the older, agrarian society whose businesses were small, local affairs.

The coming of giant corporations was profoundly unsettling, for the process not only altered the way of life of the great majority of people, but it seemed to call into question many of the ideas and values by which Americans had defined themselves and their nation. The cult of individualism, the belief in competition and in democracy, the belief that anyone could rise through his own efforts to wealth and power—all seemed threatened by the giant corporations whose influence came to be felt in virtually every city and town across the land. Of the many changes that have occurred in our history, few if any have made such a deep and lasting difference as the emergence of industrialization and its characteristic institution, the large corporation. Until recent decades, however, historians had talked a great deal about the antitrust movement but had provided relatively little in the way of thoughtful generalizations about the process by which big business actually arose.

To some extent, historical work on the coming of giant corporations has reflected the rather paradoxical way in which Americans have responded to large-scale enterprise. At the same time that the American people were upset about the rise of big business, they were also eagerly embracing it. No other country in the Western world made antitrust a prime political issue, and none has exhibited the same kind of long-run tradition of institutionalized concern about big business as has the United States. Paradoxically, few nations have created so many giant firms so quickly and have extended the bureaucratization of their economic activities so far as the United States. Americans have always admired giant economic organizations while at the same time fearing them, and the treatment of the rise of big business by American historians has reflected the conflicting popular views.

For many years, most historical assessments of the rise of big business were either emotionally slanted attacks on the "robber barons" or else attempts to refute such interpretations by focusing on the positive side of the coming of large-scale enterprises (that is, such contributions as greater productive efficiency and expanded economic growth). The first group of historians usually coupled a "liberal" or "progressive" political preference with a view of history in which the rise of big business was seen as the inevitable product of capitalism's continuous tendency toward the concentration of capital and production into larger and larger units. "If society is founded on the idea that property belongs to the strongest," Henry Demarest Lloyd argued in *Wealth Against Commonwealth* (1894), "these will sooner or later get all the property, by bargains or by battles according to 'the spirit of the age.'" Some of the better contributors to the robber baron school of historiography, such as Matthew Josephson (*The Robber Barons* [1934]), demonstrated an appreciation of the varieties and complexities of history by acknowledging the role of factors such as entrepreneurship, technology, and plain good luck in shaping the coming of big business. Rather than lingering upon explanations of the coming of big business, however, such historical works usually featured moral denunciations of the avarice and ruthlessness of big businessmen, questioning the appropriateness of the wealth and power society conferred on a relative few. Invoking the American ideals of political and economic democracy, Josephson denounced the "new nobility" whose members "organize and exploit . . . farmers and workers into harmonious corps of producers . . . only in the name of an uncontrolled appetite for private profit. . . ."

The opposing interpretation of the period was, for many years, that the business giants had made positive contributions by bringing greater efficiency and organization to the economy. This approach came to be known in some quarters as the "industrial statesmen" view. By looking at events from the perspective of the businessman, these historians naturally came to see history in terms which made all business behavior reasonable, and even praiseworthy. Sometimes this process of revisionism went to extremes, as in Julius Grodinsky's *Jay Gould* (1957). Matthew Josephson had called Gould (an unscrupulous railroad promoter in the 1870s and 1880s) "Mephistopheles"; in Grodinsky's view, Gould's schemes "performed a service to society" by encouraging competition. One could choose his political preferences, observe the era from the standpoint of the large businessmen or "the public interest," and decide whether Carnegie, Rockefeller, and the others were robber barons or industrial statesmen.

The historical treatment of the coming of big business was thus a part of the larger, twentieth-century historiographical trend toward "progressive" history. Liberal historians interpreted American history from the populist movement on as a series of conflicts between the forces of good (fighting for greater democracy and a more nearly equal distribution of wealth) and the opposing forces of conservatism (fighting to maintain the status quo). This interpretive tradition was dominant in America at least until the 1950s. Dissenters (usually called "revisionists") merely had a differing set of political views; they did not alter the prevailing view of history as a moral struggle.

The historical work of the last two decades has seriously eroded the progressive view of history. The "consensus" historians of the 1950s and 1960s emphasized the relatively narrow range of political and social disagreement in American history, and some undermined the progressive historians by pointing out the uglier sides (such as anti-Semitism, racism, and nativism) of various reform movements. Even more recently, the New Left has broken completely with progressive history's admiration of the post-industrial reform movements, denouncing the reformers for failing to bring more fundamental changes. Gabriel Kolko's *The Triumph of Conservatism* (1963), for example, painted the progressive movement as a basically conservative phenomenon heavily influenced by businessmen. The New Left has not, however, abandoned the politically influenced methods of earlier historians; their more demanding moral sieves merely produce far fewer good guys than those of their less radical predecessors.

In recent years, there has been an effort to reshape our view of the past by writing what might be called "amoral" history. Each generation of historians believes itself to be more objective and scientific than the last, and the present one is surely no exception. The decline of progressive history (and perhaps a spreading dissatisfaction with the ability of traditional mid-twentieth-century American liberalism to serve as an organizing social philosophy) has sent historians looking for new ways of doing history. Many have turned to quantification and have sought through voting analyses, demographic data, and econometric models to produce a new history which will qualify as a truly scientific "social science." Still others, drawing on sociology, organization theory, and (to a lesser extent) economics, have attempted to analyze process and structure without passing explicit moral judgments on the men and institutions of the past. This kind of work in institutional economic and business history, such as that by Alfred D. Chandler, Jr., has pointed to the relationships between the functions of an organization and its structure; his *Strategy and Structure* (1962) demonstrated that the form of a business enterprise is shaped by the nature and complexity of the tasks it performs. In the study of the rise and later development of big business, this last historical viewpoint has been especially fruitful.

This present book is framed in that institutional tradition, and the author hopes to avoid explicit moralizing. The book attempts to look at the rise of big business by examining the underlying institutional changes which made it possible, by investigating the role of markets, changing transportation and communication networks, production processes, legal environment, financial institutions, and other factors, and by posing some suggestions about the wider implications of the new, giant businesses which rose to dominance in the American economy between the Civil War and the early years of the twentieth century. By exploring these and similar questions, we may be able to reach a deeper understanding of this important part of American history than by approaching the topic in a spirit of blame or praise.

The essential first step is to be clear on what is meant by the term "big business." The purpose of this first chapter, therefore, is to provide a general definition of the nature and functions of big business; the creature will at least be surrounded if not completely subdued. It is important to understand the differences between this brand of big business and the smaller type of business firms common in America before the last half of the nineteenth century.

There are a great many kinds of businesses operating in the American economy. Major examples include: agriculture; forestry; fishing; mining; construction; manufacturing; transportation; communications; utilities; wholesale and retail trade; finance; insurance; service industries such as repair facilities and legal, medical, and educational businesses; and the operations of various governmental agencies. When Americans think of big business, however, they usually think of the large corporations engaged primarily in manufacturing—General Motors, Standard Oil, du Pont, U.S. Steel, and so on. Other kinds of businesses, of course, would also probably come to mind, firms such as United Airlines, the Chase Manhattan Bank, and American Telephone and Telegraph. In the decades after the Civil War, when people spoke of big business, they had in mind three kinds of enterprises in particular: railroads, manufacturing corporations, and banks. The men of those businesses—the Vanderbilts, Harrimans, Rockefellers, Carnegies, Dukes, Morgans, and others—symbolized the changing nature of the economy. Although other kinds of businesses, both then and later, exhibited some of the characteristics of big business, it was the "rise" of large-scale firms in those three areas (particularly in railroads and manufacturing) which signaled the coming of a new economic order in the land. Those are the industries with which most of this book will deal.

"Big business" refers (at least in this book) to a particular kind of institution through which men financed, produced, and distributed goods and services. A big business was a very different economic creation from the businesses of colonial and early national days. It was structured differently, and it did different things in new ways. These differences may be looked at from various viewpoints, but here they will be explained in terms of several basic institutional characteristics—characteristics of the structure, function, and behavior of the businesses. Most enterprises considered to be big businesses exhibited these distinctive features.

One obvious characteristic of large-scale enterprises was that they embodied very much larger pools of capital than the businesses of earlier days. The typical business establishment of the first part of the nineteenth century was financed by a single person or by several people bound together in a partnership. As such, it represented the personal wealth of a very few persons. Most manufacturing enterprises (with the exception of some textile mills and iron furnaces) were quite small, involving little in the way of physical plant or expensive machinery. It was relatively easy to get into business, for the initial costs of going into trade or simple manufacturing were within the reach of many citizens. Business failures were frequent, but there was little social or economic stigma attached to having failed unless the bankrupt man was thought dishonest; stupidity, but not deception, was repeatedly forgivable. Corporations were rare and business had a very personal tone. The fact that it was easy to enter business nurtured the belief that the society was open and fluid, that this was a land of opportunity. The goods most men bought were made and sold by small businesses, and because the capital requirements for most businesses were small, people could easily dream of owning and operating their own establishments. A great many people in antebellum America, it seemed, were in business, if only in a small way. "What most astonishes me in the United States," Alexis de Tocqueville recalled of his visit in the 1830s, "is not so much the marvelous grandeur of some undertakings, as the innumerable multitudes of small ones."

The capital represented by many of the late-nineteenth-century corporations was obviously vastly larger than even the grandest undertakings of the antebellum years. The buildings and machines of the later enterprises were numerous and expensive. The capital needed to build, maintain, and operate the many factories, warehouses, offices, distribution facilities, and other accouterments of big business was enormous. It was almost impossible to create and run such an institution without gathering money from many people. The capital represented by early giant enterprises such as Standard Oil, American Tobacco, Swift and Company, and the various large railroads amounted to many millions of dollars. For example, the excellent study of Standard Oil by two basically sympathetic revisionist historians (Ralph and Muriel Hidy's *Pioneering in Big Business, 1882–1911* [1955]) showed the company's net book value in 1910 to be in excess of 600 million dollars. And when U.S. Steel was created in 1901, the news which most amazed and impressed contemporaries was the fact that the firm was capitalized at over one billion dollars. By way of comparison, the capital represented by even the largest of antebellum manufacturers—the textile companies—was less than a million dollars, and the vast majority of firms engaged in factory production before 1860 were much smaller. The coming of giant corporations soon altered the old assumption that almost anyone could go into his own business and have some chance of succeeding as well as anyone else. A man would surely have been thought a lunatic in 1901 if he sat around planning the creation of, say, another U.S. Steel with the savings and credit of a few friends.

Another important difference between small and large businesses was related to the scale of capital needs just discussed. This related distinction lay in the differing nature of capital needs and costs for small and large firms. A business needed two kinds of capital, fixed and working, and it encountered two kinds of costs, fixed (or constant) and operating (or variable). Put in a highly simplified way, fixed capital or assets were those represented by a company's land, buildings, and machinery; working capital was the money needed to run the business once it was in operation. Fixed (or constant) costs were those borne by the firm whether it was producing or not—such as interest charges on the fixed capital, taxes, and so on. Operating costs, on the other hand, were represented by salaries, wages, raw materials, and any associated direct costs of production, distribution, and transportation. The small manufacturers of the first half of the nineteenth century found that their yearly operating costs were very high, often exceeding the initial cost of the land and physical plant. That is, working capital was much more important than fixed capital for most early businessmen. Merchants and small artisan-entrepreneurs had even less in the way of fixed capital and fixed costs. When a depression or recession struck, it was not hard for a firm to ride it out simply by closing down temporarily and sending the workers home. "When an article was produced by a small manufacturer, employing, probably at his own home, two or three journeymen and an apprentice or two," Andrew Carnegie wrote in an 1889 magazine article, "it was an easy matter for him to limit or even to stop production." Because the physical plant did not represent much capital, it did not disturb an owner greatly to see it lying idle. Even if the money tied up in the idle factory were invested in securities or loaned to others, the interest it would have earned would not have been very much. Because the operating costs were so high and the constant costs relatively low, antebellum firms had considerable control over when and under what circumstances they would continue to do business.

The cost structure of big businesses was quite different. Part of the story of the coming of large-scale enterprise was advancing technology, which made factory production possible in many industries and which brought new processes in the manufacture of metals, petroleum, chemicals, electrical products, automobiles, and other items. The new giant firms utilized complex technologies and many factories, and they did so because the new productive techniques made it possible to turn out huge quantities of goods at a lower cost per item. However, the coming of complex technology had significant effects on the structure of fixed costs for the firms involved. The many factories, mills, refineries, blast furnaces, and assembly lines represented enormous amounts of capital, and these firms experienced much higher constant costs than had their antebellum predecessors. Because the fixed costs amounted to such vast sums (and also because it was often technically very difficult to shut down and then start up again), they found it much more costly to cease production just because business was bad. "As manufacturing is carried on today [1889]," the steel king Carnegie argued in the *North American Review,* "in enormous establishments with five or ten millions of dollars of capital invested, and with thousands of workers, it costs the manufacturer much less to run at a loss per ton or per yard than to check his production. Stoppage would be serious indeed. . . . Therefore the article is produced for months [or] for years . . . without profit or without interest on capital." Such high-cost, technologically advanced industries depended on fairly steady levels of operation to achieve low costs per unit of output, and this factor proved a significant determinant of economic behavior and the rise of big business, as we will see later.

These comments about the capital needs and costs of a big business point to another related and significant difference which existed between it and the smaller institutions of the past. This distinction was the altered nature of ownership. The business enterprises of the early United States were usually owned by one or several individuals, often bound together by ties of kinship and marriage. This familial aspect of antebellum businesses traced its lineage back to the earliest colonial days, as Bernard Bailyn's investigation of *The New England Merchants in the Seventeenth Century* (1955) indicated. Normally the owners of a business were also its managers. The owner-entrepreneurs made all the key decisions about the conduct of their firms. They knew intimately the needs and mode of operation of their businesses. They brought their sons, nephews, or talented in-laws into their firms to learn the details of the business, and when a firm's management changed, so often did its ownership. Almost all antebellum businesses fit this pattern, from the smallest storekeepers to the richest and most powerful families, such as the Browns in Rhode Island and the Hancocks, Lowells, and Appletons in Massachusetts. Because of the intensely personal nature of ownership and control, these early businesses often died with the passing of the owner or the lack of interest or absence of talent among the surviving males in the family.

Big businesses functioned with another method of ownership altogether. As economists A. A. Berle and Gardiner Means pointed out early in the 1930s in a book since enshrined as "a classic study" (*The Modern Corporation and Private Property* [1934]), a hallmark of the modern business enterprise was its separation of ownership and control. Because huge pools of capital were necessary, ownership usually had to be dispersed among a great many people, and that in turn meant that the owner-entrepreneur commonly had no place in the new kind of enterprise. As the primary organizational form changed from partnership to corporation around the turn of the century, the number of owners (shareholders) grew so large that they had to turn over control of the business to one man or a few men. And as the complexity of management grew, the corporations eventually came to be run by professionals who had little or no actual ownership in the firms they controlled. It became increasingly rare, especially after the beginning of the twentieth century, for the ownership and management of a major firm to remain in the hands of a single family. William Miller, in a study of the leaders of giant business enterprises in the period from 1901 to 1910 (published in a collection of essays, *Men in Business* [1962]), found that the majority were either managers who had risen through the company bureaucracy or outside professionals with special skills, such as lawyers. Once ownership was widely spread and management became the job of skilled, professional businessmen, the firm was freed from its old dependence on the money, talent, and health of any one man or group of men. It became a virtually immortal institution, easily surviving the deaths of owners and the onset of incompetence or disinterest in any single family. Once these changes occurred, businesses increasingly became anonymous, impersonal institutions. The rise of big business inevitably brought with it these fundamental changes in the nature and control of property in America.

It also meant sweeping alterations in the spatial or geographical scale on which businesses operated. In the simpler world before large-scale enterprises, many firms operated in a single town or city, or at least from a single office or factory. Almost all manufacturing companies sold their goods in two ways. Some sales went to customers in the immediate area, and the rest of the product was sold through merchants in a nearby major city. For example, Baltimore iron merchant Enoch Pratt (whose generosity later founded that city's excellent public library system) sold the goods made by numerous manufacturers in Maryland, West Virginia, and Pennsylvania on the eve of the Civil War. The typical manufacturer had a very limited horizon; he often lived out his days in ignorance of events and people in distant parts of the country. Retailers exhibited a similar insularity. There were, of course, some businessmen whose work did require a knowledge of affairs over a broader area; merchants who dealt in international trade had existed since the Middle Ages, and in the American context, bankers and merchants acted as the connecting and coordinating units in the economy. Such businessmen had to function in a wide geographic context, extending credit, making collections, buying, and selling. The banking house of Alexander Brown and Sons, for example, assisted commercial transactions all over the world from their branches in New York, Baltimore, and other cities in the decades before the election of Abraham Lincoln. Beginning in the colonial years and the first few decades after the conclusion of the Revolutionary War, the general merchants of the seaboard cities, such as South Carolina's Henry Laurens, dealt with people all over the country and around the world. Despite that, their enterprises were not big businesses, but were instead very successful small ones, usually involving only a few men. Very few manufacturers, retailers, or others had substantial contacts outside the immediate area in which they did business.

This situation was overturned completely by the rise of big business. The giant enterprise of the turn of the century carried out its functions in a great many different, widely scattered locations. The old pattern of a single factory per firm gave way to an array of productive facilities. As they expanded their activities, manufacturing firms and railroads found their names becoming household words (often preceded by barroom adjectives) in states all over the union. The railroads laid their tracks and ran their trains over long distances, single roads or systems eventually covering hundreds of miles and many states. Manufacturing corporations came to have numerous plants for the production of their goods, and later when individual firms diversified into various product lines, the number and kinds of factories, mills, and refineries per firm were still further increased. As manufacturing corporations took over some of the functions that had earlier belonged to independent businesses (functions such as wholesaling, transportation, and sometimes retailing), they operated in more and more widely scattered locales. For example, by 1900 General Electric had numerous plants in various locations and had sales offices in twenty-three cities across the country. By the early years of this century, as Mira Wilkins has shown in her *American Enterprise Abroad* (1970), many large corporations had extended their business activities around the world. Muckraking cartoonists at the turn of the century often depicted the leading business giants of the day as spiders whose webs enveloped vast areas, ever ready to trap the unwary or the helpless. As the cartoons indicated, this new spatial dimension of business was particularly disturbing to Americans accustomed to the older world of local, small, single-plant enterprises; big business, like the Deity the citizens addressed on Sundays, seemed to be everywhere.

Not only did the coming of big business mean that private economic enterprises carried out their functions on a much enlarged geographic landscape, but it also meant that they engaged in many more kinds of business operations than had earlier firms. Although the great colonial seaport merchants had handled a wide range of activities in the early economy, they were supplanted by a new kind of business after 1815, when mercantile operations became more highly specialized. A merchant tended to become primarily a wholesaler or retailer, an exporter or an importer, one particular kind of mercantile businessman rather than a mixture of several. Furthermore, wholesalers often specialized in a single line of goods such as drugs, dry goods, hardware, or other articles. "By 1860," George Rogers Taylor wrote in *The Transportation Revolution, 1815–1860* (1951), "the organization of both foreign and domestic trade had reached a high degree of specialization."

Specialization had been even more characteristic of manufacturing operations. Manufacturers, whether small artisans or the owners of early factories, were specialized in function and in product; they were usually only producers and ordinarily made only a single kind of item or a small number of similar goods. For example, an iron furnace of the 1850s normally made only pig (cast) iron; it did not convert the cast iron into semi-finished wrought iron or into finished products such as nails or hardware. Separate businesses handled the processing of the cast iron—businesses such as forges, slitting mills, and rolling mills, all of which had no direct connection with the furnace. But in a big business such as Carnegie Steel in 1900, one firm made cast iron and steel plus a wide variety of other metal goods in its own rolling mills and forges. When a mid-nineteenth-century manufacturer needed to market his products, he had turned to specialized wholesalers who handled the task of merchandising the goods to distant retailers or other customers. When he needed to have his goods transported, he had called on forwarding merchants or on the early traffic departments of railroads. For example, an ironmaster of 1850 would simply turn over the marketing of his pig iron to a separate businessman (an iron merchant like Baltimore's Enoch Pratt) who sold the goods and charged the ironmaster for his services. Carnegie Steel, on the other hand, had its own company sales force by 1900. Similarly, in the business of raising, butchering, transporting, and selling fresh meat, each step in 1850 had been handled by a different, separate business. By 1900, firms such as Swift and Armour were doing slaughtering, transportation, and wholesaling of beef all as a part of the same company's operations. The economic world of the United States in the mid-nineteenth century was highly subdivided, and each business did its special task with little knowledge of related activities.

The modern manufacturing corporation altered that earlier world by expanding the range of a firm's functions and its products. Big businesses often combined under a single corporate roof the activities of obtaining raw materials, of turning them into manufactured products, of wholesaling the goods, and sometimes of retailing them, as Glenn Porter and Harold C. Livesay have demonstrated by examining a number of major corporations in *Merchants and Manufacturers* (1971). Many corporations also came to have their own internal traffic departments which handled the transportation of goods, sometimes via the companies' own fleets of trucks, ships, or railroad cars (Swift & Co. and Standard Oil are good examples). And many large businesses were also able to achieve a high degree of autonomy in the financial sphere as well, paying for improvements or new operations out of earlier earnings retained by the corporations, or issuing stocks or bonds whose acceptance rested more on the strength of the business than on the reputation of the bankers who underwrote the issues. In 1850 such financial independence was rare. An ironmaster or meatpacker had to rely for loans on separate businesses such as banks or big wholesalers. Antebellum merchants often loaned substantial amounts to manufacturers, and some merchants eventually transferred their skills into the field of banking, as illustrated by Elva Tooker's study of a Philadelphia metal merchant, *Nathan Trotter* (1955). By 1900, however, firms like Carnegie Steel and Armour & Co. were strong enough to be independent of such outside financial help.

The coming of big business saw an accumulation of various different economic functions within a single company (often called vertical integration), and unification made business units much more powerful and much more the masters of their own economic fate. Big businessmen found themselves freer to act and more able to control the course of their enterprises with "everything being within ourselves," as Andrew Carnegie once phrased it. As they multiplied their functions, so too did large-scale enterprises increase their range of products. Giant businesses abandoned the traditional pattern of narrow specialization and turned to the production of several different kinds of goods, especially as the twentieth century progressed. Long before the word "conglomerate" appeared, American business had learned to apply its talents and productive facilities to a diversity of products within a single firm.

The proliferation of factories, the geographical growth of firms, the increasing variety of products, and most especially the accumulation of different types of economic functions within an enterprise necessitated a complete change in the way businesses were run. In the days before giant enterprises, businesses required very little in the way of administrative networks. Mercantile, commercial, and financial enterprises usually involved only a few partners and a handful of clerks who had a knowledge of bookkeeping and could write in the flowing, clear, formal business penmanship so useful in avoiding misunderstandings in the pre-typewriter age. The small manufacturing shops peopled by an artisan-entrepreneur and a few workers or apprentices likewise required little in the way of administration. Even the factories which arose before the Civil War involved only a manager, a few foremen, and a group of workers who normally all labored in the same building. Under such circumstances, it was easy for an owner or manager to oversee personally almost all the operations in his business. When something went wrong or could be improved, the boss had only to shout out his wishes to the few men who took orders from him. Similarly, because businesses seldom operated in more than one location, there were almost no problems of controlling distant operations. The only groups of businessmen who normally did business in widely separated areas, the large merchants and bankers, tried to insure accountability and honesty in distant branches by staffing them with relatives. Few concerns, however, had any problems with the administration of the firm or factory; such issues rarely arose before the advent of large-scale corporations.

As big businesses appeared in the economy, however, new administrative problems appeared, and new managerial patterns became necessary. How could an owner or manager know what was going on in the various locales? How could he make his decisions known to distant employees and see that they were effectively carried out? As the number of different kinds of functions performed by a single firm increased, the difficulties grew even more complex. How could the needs and capacities of the various divisions of the firm be ascertained and coordinated? How could the purchasing department supply the right amount and kinds of raw material in the right sequence to be sure the factories or mills could function efficiently? How could the marketing activities be geared to the rate of production so as to insure a rational flow of goods into the market and thus avoid fluctuations in prices and profits? The success of the venture depended on a great many separate but interrelated activities, all of which had to be managed well to see that the internal rhythm of the enterprise was intelligently controlled and coordinated. Everything was connected with something else, and it was all scattered about the landscape so that no one man could possibly oversee the operation personally.

The solutions to the new and perplexing problems of management could only be found through the creation of elaborate, formal administrative networks, the bureaucracies which are the characteristic organizational form of the twentieth century. To work efficiently, business had to be carefully organized, with various levels of managers making and implementing both the long-range planning for the venture as a whole and the day-to-day operations of its far-flung divisions. Formal, written rules were created to govern affairs ranging from the selection of qualified personnel to the operation of the production and distribution processes to the procedures for firing vice-presidents and janitors. Clear lines of authority and control had to be devised so that people understood their roles, responsibilities, authority, and accountability. Only by building such an elaborate administrative network was it possible for big businesses to avoid chaos.

When businessmen began creating large-scale enterprises in the last half of the nineteenth century, they were usually unaware of these problems at first. Often the result was indeed chaotic. Rather than reaping the benefits of large-scale operations, they sometimes found themselves encountering losses as a result of their inability to solve complex managerial problems efficiently. The transition to big business was often a troubled, painful, experimental process which produced more failures than successes. Many prominent railroads had gone bankrupt and been reorganized several times by the 1890s, and many of the early combinations in manufacturing were complete failures. Because the institution of big business was new, the men who built large corporations had to feel their way through the early years. Because they were trying something new, they had no source for informed and experienced assistance. Only after businesses had arisen whose size and complexity called for correspondingly large and involved bureaucratic managerial structures did universities create graduate management schools in the first decade of the twentieth century to train people to run big businesses. Management became a very different and considerably more involved job after the rise of large-scale business concerns, and the likelihood of a single manager's running such a venture efficiently became very small indeed.

As large corporations began to build the elaborate bureaucracies necessary for their existence, another profound difference between the mid-nineteenth-century concern and the turn-of-the-century giant enterprise emerged—business began to lose its highly personal tone. Almost from the earliest days of economic endeavors among the European colonists, businesses were extensions of the personalities of the men who ran them. The way in which businesses dealt with other businesses—with assurance and respect or with misgivings and extreme caution—depended on the personal character and personal wealth of individuals. In large part, this was due to the fact that very few concerns were widely owned or were organized in corporate form. A business was worth only as much as its owner or his partners, and business success rested heavily on how others perceived one's character. Because the entire early economy functioned on credit (few were able to pay cash, and payment after six, twelve, or eighteen months was common), the confidence of creditors in a man often determined his ability to expand during good times or to survive in bad times. The whole ethos of nineteenth-century individualism and what today seems small-town morality was closely related to this cluster of attitudes and values toward business. When Lewis Tappan founded his Mercantile Agency in the 1840s (the country's first nationwide credit bureau), the credit rating of a business was influenced almost as much by the character and personal habits of its owners as by the firm's profits, assets, and future prospects. The good businessman was sober, honest, diligent, hardworking, and shrewd—an amalgam of the old puritan virtues harnessed in pursuit of profit. He did not hang around saloons or associate with loose women—or at least he did so with the same discretion and shrewdness he brought to his leatherbound journals and day books. Firms were merely the forms in which individuals cloaked themselves to do business; as an antebellum phrase put it, a firm's name was merely the current "style" of a businessman. Perhaps the clearest indication of the personal tone of business was the fact that it was common for a firm to die with the death of its owner.

Relationships between owner-managers and their workers were also quite personal. Because the manager saw his few employees frequently and lived with them in the same town, he could at least be expected to know their names, the quality of their work, and perhaps even some things about their personal lives. The nature of relationships between the labor force and the managers, as well as the highly individual identification of persons with their firms, underwent considerable change in the big businesses which had evolved by the turn of the century.

A necessary concomitant of bureaucracy was impersonality; a complex administrative network created a social and economic gap between men on various levels of the hierarchy. As the operations of a single business grew larger, more involved, and more widely separated, individual employees often had no knowledge of the distant, almost disembodied people who controlled and manipulated the business and thus their lives. As more and more technologically advanced production processes appeared, work became mechanized and routinized. Many workers had little or no understanding of their part in the overall operations of the giant organization, little sense of accomplishment or participation beyond their particular, distinct task. Work itself, as well as one's relations with others in the organization, grew increasingly impersonal.

This impersonality spread to the owners and managers as well. As ownership was diffused among many people via incorporation and public purchase of stock, businesses began to lose their aura of identification with an individual owner or with several partners. Corporations became virtually immortal institutions whose owners could not easily be identified. As professional managers with little or no ownership rose to positions of power in the corporate world, many firms assumed an air of anonymity and impersonality. The importance of character and individual reliability in business dealings diminished as firms assumed a life of their own apart from those of the men who staffed and served them. As anyone who has ever dealt with a modern bureaucracy understands, one could no longer simply go in and settle a dispute or misunderstanding by exchanging some straight talk with the owner. The locus of power and responsibility often seemed as elusive as the Cheshire cat in Wonderland, despite (and, paradoxically, also because of) the elaborate rules, the standardized procedures, and the supposedly clear lines of authority and responsibility.

The years of the rise of big business did not, alas, present an entirely clear picture of the shift from a highly personal to a very impersonal business world. As is always the case, events do not conform easily to the generalizations historians produce to try to make sense of the past. The particular problem at hand is that the years 1860–1910 seemed also in many ways to be the most highly personalized era in the history of American business. During the transitional period between the origins of firms that became modern giant enterprises and the subsequent triumph of diffused ownership and professional managers, there emerged that fascinating generation of individuals so intimately associated in the public mind with the coming of big business. The era of the "trusts" was conceptualized by Americans of the time (and by many later historians) in terms of the men who symbolized the early giant corporations—men like John D. Rockefeller, Gustavus Swift, Philip Armour, James Duke, Henry Havemeyer, Andrew Carnegie, William Vanderbilt, and the biggest and boldest of them all, John Pierpont Morgan.

It is not hard to understand why it seemed an age of business titans, robber barons, and industrial giants. First, there was considerable justification for thinking of the corporations in terms of the men, at least for a time. The men usually held a large chunk of ownership, if not a controlling interest, and many of them did play important managerial roles in their enterprises. Furthermore, it seems to be a universal human trait to adopt the mental shorthand of identifying if possible a single individual with the larger entity of which he is a part, especially if the entity is thought to be evil; Hitler symbolized all of Nazi Germany, the Bank of the United States was "Biddle's Bank," and so on. The large railroads and the pioneering manufacturing corporations such as Standard Oil, American Sugar, American Tobacco, and others seemed even larger than life and even more awesomely powerful than they actually were simply because they were the first such institutions Americans had witnessed. They were novel and unfamiliar, and the men who symbolized them seemed all the more mysteriously grand and ominously impressive as a result.

Of course, in no case did any of the famous business giants really control directly most of the numerous and varied activities of the enterprises associated with their names. It was impossible for the man at the top to penetrate very far into a complex bureaucracy; the operation depended on many people. And the men who provided the initial innovative idea or the leadership to launch a big business often found their degree of ownership and control diminishing as the concerns grew. James Duke, for example, found his control over American Tobacco slipping into the hands of outside bankers and financiers well before the government's successful antitrust suit was completed in 1911. After a national market arose for industrial securities in the 1890s, and as management increasingly became the province of skilled professionals, even the public vision of big business leaders began to blur. In reality, the generation of giants (the lords of creation, Frederick Lewis Allen called some of them) acted as midwives in the birth of modern corporations. The achievements of these men were considerable, their talents great, and their fortunes enormous. But if they had not called forth the new institution of large-scale business enterprise, others would have, for its time had clearly come. In this sense, their personal stamp on the era is illusory, for the businesses they began quickly outgrew their ability to control or manage them. The impersonal, institutional demands of giant firms shaped new patterns of ownership and management by the opening years of the twentieth century, eclipsing the brief but bright glow of the men whose names had for a time symbolized big business.

Whether the giant corporations were personal or impersonal, a final aspect of big businesses which should be noted is that they represented very great conglomerations of wealth and power. Although the business world before 1850 produced some extremely rich individuals and some influential companies, it contained nothing comparable to the accumulated wealth and power embodied in the huge firms of the late nineteenth and early twentieth century. Decisions made by the managers of giant enterprises affected the lives of thousands and could affect the course of the economy as a whole. A few men became rich on a scale never before possible, and they enjoyed the influence that follows from such wealth. Although it is very difficult to judge whether the influence of business as a whole in American life was increased (it had always been great), there is little doubt that the rise of big business meant the concentration of economic and social power in the hands of a very few. Fear of that power and its relative immunity from the democratic process in the political sphere contributed mightily to the misgivings that Americans felt about the new economic institutions that arose in their society from 1850 to 1910.

The purpose of this chapter has been to examine those institutions and to describe a big business in terms of its structure and functions. Only by examining the contrasting nature of business institutions before and after the rise of big business is it possible to understand the magnitude of the economic changes during the years covered in this book. A large-scale business enterprise, as we have seen, differed substantially from earlier businesses in terms of several characteristics: its capital requirements; its high fixed costs; the nature of its ownership; the geographic scale on which it operated; its performance of various different economic functions embodied in a range of goods and services; its managerial and administrative needs; its anonymity and impersonality; and its great power and wealth. There were other hallmarks of the giant business concerns that could be listed, but the ones already discussed should serve to explain what big business was, how it worked, and how it represented a new institution in the American economy.

The coming of those new economic institutions collectively known as big business had many fundamental and far-reaching implications for American society. The effects on our political history were immediate; much of the bitter conflict associated with populism, progressivism, and the New Deal resulted from the rise and spread of big businesses and from disagreements over the proper role of such institutions in American life. The emergence of other great institutions, especially organized labor and "big" government, can also be seen as basically political responses to the rise of big business, as John Kenneth Galbraith argued in his *American Capitalism: The Concept of Countervailing Power* (1952). Indeed, as was pointed out early in this chapter, much of the work historians have done on the topic of large-scale business enterprises has revolved around their specifically political significance. In a larger sense, however, the rise of big business was only the most obvious manifestation of a broad range of economic and social changes which resulted in the emergence of modern America.

In the era of the Civil War, the United States was still very clearly a rural, agrarian-based civilization. By the early decades of this century, the nation was just as clearly transformed into an urban, industrial civilization. The advent of giant, bureaucratically administered, highly productive corporations brought for most Americans changes in the nature of work, in the general environment in which they made their homes and secured their livelihoods, in the level of their consumption of material goods, and in the quality of their lives. The nation remade itself to accommodate to the requirements of the modern corporation. People left the country and moved to the city, with all the changes that made in their daily lives, to derive what they saw as benefits from the new patterns of working and living. If, as Richard Hofstadter once suggested, the most important fact about this nation's history is that it grew up in the country and moved to the city, it is vital to recall why the move was made. Americans embraced the new industrial order primarily because they saw it as a more promising environment in terms of their material well-being and the possibilities for economic and social mobility. Much good as well as much that was not good has flowed from the emergence of our industrial, urban nation. Whatever one's view of the ultimate worth or shortcomings of the particular kind of society we have built, it is clear that the modern corporation lies at the heart of twentieth-century American civilization. Until we understand how and why we came to have that particular institution, we cannot fully understand our society or intelligently judge the desirability and the possibility of change.

TWO

The Appearance and Spread of Big Business

THE ADVENT OF INDUSTRIALIZATION

When General Pierre Gustave Toutant Beauregard ordered the shelling of Fort Sumter in Charleston's harbor in the spring of 1861, there was only one industry in the country which included firms that could legitimately be called big businesses in the sense in which the term was used in the preceding chapter. That industry was the railroads, and at that point in our national history, they were still widely regarded as an almost unalloyed good. By the time of the Supreme Court's dissolution of Standard Oil and American Tobacco a half-century later, much of the American economy was dominated by big businesses. They had come slowly at first, appearing here and there in manufacturing by the 1880s, touching off the passage of the Sherman Antitrust Act in 1890. The depression of the mid-1890s slowed them for a time, but then they came in a torrent in the last years of the nineteenth century and the first years of the twentieth.

For a time, historians felt that the Civil War itself had played a key role in bringing about the transition to an industrialized economy with giant corporations. Charles and Mary Beard, in their *Rise of American Civilization* (1927), called the war the "second American revolution." They saw the conflict primarily as a social and economic phenomenon in which the planter aristocracy of the South was driven from national power by the expanding industrial interests of the North and West. In the Beards' view, the war gave a powerful thrust to the Industrial Revolution in America. Matthew Josephson followed that interpretation in his *Robber Barons,* and so did many others. Harold Faulkner's 1950s text *American Economic History* found the war "extremely important" as a source of speedier industrial development. In recent years, however, the economic importance of that great conflict has been severely questioned. Thomas C. Cochran, one of the nation's finest historians, touched off a controversy when he asked, "Did the Civil War Retard Industrialization?" (*Mississippi Valley Historical Review,* September 1961) and answered "yes." Others who hastened to join Cochran emphasized that America was well on the way to industrialization prior to the war, and that the events which so excited political and military historians had little discernible effect on the long-run growth of the nation's economy. Such was the general conclusion reached by the scholars whose views appeared in *Economic Change in the Civil War Era* (1965), edited by David T. Gilchrist and W. David Lewis.

It is important here to keep in mind the distinction between big business on the one hand and industrialization and the factory system on the other. The United States had begun to experience an industrial revolution before the appearance of large, bureaucratically administered firms. From the days of the War of 1812, the textile industry had operated what can surely be called modern factories. Francis Cabot Lowell founded the Boston Manufacturing Company in 1813, and that firm created in Waltham, Massachusetts, America's first textile mill combining spinning and weaving operations within a single factory. As Caroline Ware indicated in her book *Early New England Cotton Manufacture* (1931), similar "Lowell Mills" spread to other parts of New England where water power was available. In the initial decades after the passage of the Constitution, early factories appeared in other industries as well. Along the lovely Brandywine River in Delaware appeared the water-driven gunpowder mills of what was later to become one of the country's largest corporations, the du Pont company. Borrowing technological processes developed in Europe, Thomas Gilpin built an early paper mill using the force of that same river in Delaware. The nation's infant iron industry grew with the proliferation of self-contained industrial villages known as "iron plantations." Many of these, like the industrial community described in Joseph Walker's *Hopewell Village* (1966), were located in Pennsylvania.

By the 1840s, the factory had begun to spread to other industries as well. Although American producers were slow to adopt both steam technology and the advances in ironmaking under way in Britain by the 1830s, the decades of the 1840s and the 1850s saw the quick diffusion of steam power and great progress in the metalworking industries. As steam became available as a source of power for manufacturing, businessmen could locate factories in new places, sites which did not have sources of water power. This made it easier for producers to operate near urban centers which offered a large labor force or a potentially large market; similarly, manufacturers could choose sites closer to raw material sources if they so desired. The factory form of production appeared in the two decades before the

Civil War in many metalworking industries such as those manu-facturing farm implements, kitchen goods, reapers, firearms, clocks, sewing machines, and other items. While the nation in 1860 was still largely agricultural and commercial, the factory system was already well established.

By 1860 the United States was thus well launched into industrialization and rapid, sustained economic growth. Walt Rostow argued in *The Stages of Economic Growth* (1960) that this country had achieved a "take-off," a burst of expansion which touched off steady growth. Rostow dated this "great watershed" for the United States in the years 1842–1860. Econ-omists and economic historians have since directed an astonish-ing amount of work at attempting either to deny the existence of such a short burst (arguing instead that steady growth was achieved slowly, over longer time spans) or trying to move the "take-off" to an earlier period, usually the 1820s or 1830s. Economist Henry Rosovsky described the resulting raging de-bate as a "take-off into sustained controversy." Whether Ros-tow's style of take-off existed or not, and whatever years it may have graced, virtually all scholars are agreed that the nation was well on the road to industrialization and continuous, long-term economic growth by 1860.

Despite the national progress toward industrialization, how-ever, the coming of factories did not immediately result in the appearance of big businesses in manufacturing. Even the largest manufacturing operations on the 1850s (mostly textile mills and iron "plantations") did not fit the pattern sketched out in the last chapter. Only a few of the biggest manufacturing firms had capital requirements approaching one million dollars; the vast majority were much smaller. There were no manufacturing oper-ations of such magnitude as to include factories or offices scat-tered over several states or abroad. Working capital was still of great importance relative to fixed capital. Business continued to be done in single-plant operations, ownership of individual units was still concentrated among small numbers of people, ownership and management still usually went hand in hand, manufacturers specialized in a single product or a single line of goods, and industry had not yet become the province of complex, bureaucratically administered managerial networks. Almost all citizens still shared a belief in the overriding desirability of material growth, and the political controversy over the power of big businessmen still lay in the future. Of all the economic institutions on the American scene in 1860, only the railroads qualified as big businesses, and even their political difficulties lay ahead.

PIONEERS IN BIG BUSINESS: THE RAILROADS

Railroads brought new methods of management, new forms of corporate finance, different dimensions in labor relations, new ways of competition, and a new relationship between business and government. In his *The Railroads: The Nation's First Big Business* (1965), Alfred D. Chandler, Jr. made a strong case for the pathbreaking role of railroads in meeting and resolving many of the problems later faced by other giant industrial enterprises. The importance of the railroads as promoters of national economic expansion has, however, been sharply and ingeniously questioned by recent practitioners of quantitative and highly theoretical economic history. Robert W. Fogel's *Railroads and American Economic Growth* (1964) denied that the iron horse was "indispensable" to economic growth and suggested that an effective alternative transportation network could have been achieved if canals rather than railroads had been built. Albert Fishlow's *American Railroads and the Transformation of the Ante-Bellum Economy* (1965) argued for a larger economic role for the railroads than Fogel had indicated, and a great many economic historians joined in to create a ballooning controversy. Attempts to measure the railroad's contribution to national output soon degenerated into disagreements over what constituted a large or a small number, and the issue remains unclear, especially when the apocalyptic notion of "indispensability" is abandoned for some lesser word such as "importance." Despite all the cannonading, all the conflicting assumptions and econometric models, Chandler's case for the railroads as prototypes of large-scale industrial corporations has remained persuasive. However much the roads that appeared after the pioneering Baltimore and Ohio began operations in 1830 did or did not contribute to the nation's economic output, the railroads clearly led the way in the development of institutional arrangements and management practices which later appeared in big businesses in the manufacturing sector.

In the financial sphere, for example, the railroads presented problems on a scale never faced before in the United States. During the railroad construction of the 1830s, this new form of transportation, like many canals earlier in the century, had relied on heavy financial aid from state governments. The depression of the late 1830s and early 1840s, however, severely affected the states' purses and credit ratings, and the great railroad expansion of the 1850s had to proceed with less government assistance. The growth of railroads in that decade put unprecedented strains on the economy's ability to mobilize capital. In the ten years after 1850, the nation's railroad mileage tripled from 9,000 to over 30,000 miles. By the end of that decade, Henry Varnum Poor's *History of the Railroads and Canals of the United States of America* (1860) showed that numerous companies had capital accounts of over ten million dollars; several, including the New York Central, the Baltimore and Ohio, and the New York and Erie, were valued at more than twenty million. Most of the money to finance the growth of the rail system came from private investors, though some support came from the federal government and from states, cities, and counties eager to encourage transportation. Never before in the country's history had such funds been required for economic ventures; even the most expensive canal, New York's Erie, had cost only about seven million.

The result of this new demand for capital was that America's money and investment markets were centralized where they have remained since—on Wall Street. The stocks and bonds of railroads all over the country began to be listed and actively traded on the New York Stock Exchange as the capital of investors in this country and in Europe was mobilized in support of railways. At the same time, the modern investment banking house appeared to handle the marketing of the new securities. The earliest firm to provide the services now associated with investment banking, Winslow, Lanier & Co., began in New York in 1849 and flourished on the negotiation of railroad securities, as Vincent Carosso pointed out in his *Investment Banking in America* (1970). In the 1850s, Carosso noted, such companies "contributed substantially toward making New York City the principal center of American railroad finance." As we will see later, a similar revolution in the nation's capital markets in the 1890s permitted and encouraged the flood of large industrial combinations around the turn of the century. The railroads, however, were the first businesses to require such large amounts that the savings of men from all over this country and abroad had to be marshaled.

The complexity of railroads' operations also forced them to face and resolve new managerial, as well as financial, difficulties. A large railroad's activities extended over hundreds of miles and involved enormous problems of planning, coordination, and control. The number of financial transactions handled by a road's conductors, station agents, and freight agents required a central controller's office, begun first by the B & O. The scheduling of the flow of equipment to match expected demand over the system also called for new managerial structures. The long- and short-term capital needs of the giant enterprises had to be carefully planned, and the railroads became the first businesses to achieve modern cost analysis or cost accounting to measure the firm's performance and to aid in setting rates. These and other problems, on both a day-to-day and a long-term basis, called forth bureaucratically structured administrative networks to manage the huge, complex activities of the railroads. No manufacturing firm faced such difficulties until later in the nineteenth century, and when they did arise in other industries, most firms turned to the management experience of the railroads as a guide. The railroads proved a fertile training ground for men who later ran big businesses in the manufacturing sector; Andrew Carnegie was probably the most famous railroad "graduate" to go on to another large-scale enterprise. When graduate schools of business administration appeared in this country shortly before the outbreak of World War I, the managerial principles derived from the experience of the railroads played an important role in their programs.

In some ways, the railroads were also leaders in forging new patterns of labor relations. Their workers were the first to operate in an impersonal, bureaucratically controlled environment, and they were the first to achieve genuine collective bargaining and grievance channels through their national unions, the railroad brotherhoods. Initially these unions, like many other early American labor organizations, were social and mutual benefit societies. By the 1870s, though, they were evolving into modern unions. Like many of the craft unions which formed the American Federation of Labor in the 1880s, the railway brotherhoods derived their economic strength from the fact that their members had scarce and hard to replace skills. A strike by such a union was a real threat to employers, because it was extremely difficult to break the strike by bringing in outside workers ("scabs" in union parlance). Furthermore, the railway workers were additionally vital because they controlled the use and maintenance of expensive equipment. The unhappy history of unions that tried to include all the nation's working people, such as the National Labor Union and the Knights of Labor, indicated that it was very difficult, if not impossible, to create and maintain unions unless the members had scarce economic skills like the railroad workers and the members of the craft unions that made up the American Federation of Labor in the 1880s. The all-inclusive unions faced other difficulties as well. Gerald Grob's *Workers and Utopia* (1961) convincingly argued that the members and the leaders of such non-craft unions shared an ideological reluctance to accept the wage system, an economic arrangement which conflicted with Americans' strong desires for their own businesses. This essentially middle class or petit bourgeois outlook was revealed in the declaration of Terence Powderly, the leader of the Knights, that "the aim of the Knights of Labor . . . is to make each man his own employer." Unions based on that principle had little chance of attaining the success that marked the railroad brotherhoods.

The giant corporations which arose in manufacturing, moreover, were more successful in fighting off unionization than were the railways. Most of the new big businesses came in industries which relied on semi-skilled rather than skilled workers, and here unions found it extremely difficult to make any headway. Not until the New Deal, when the Wagner Act gave legal status to democratically chosen collective bargaining units (unions) and brought the power of the federal government to bear on employers, were industrial big businesses participants in the kind of labor relations found on the railroads in the late nineteenth century.

The railroads also were the first businesses to face new and severe problems of competition. As the first chapter pointed out, most big businesses had high constant costs—costs that persisted even when the firm was not operating or was running at very low levels of production. The railroads provided an early and quite striking example of this situation. Not only did their equipment and roads prove very costly (representing many millions in capital), but in addition, most railroads had a very large debt in the form of bonds. When the railroad expansion of the 1850s occurred, much of the money raised in the capital markets was obtained through the sale of bonds rather than stock. At least until the 1890s, investors preferred bonds to stock because they thought of the bonds as sounder securities. Interest on bonds normally had first legal call on any profits of the business, and investors therefore looked on them as much more reliable sources of income than stocks. As a result, railroads borrowed enormous sums in the 1850s and in later decades through the sale of bonds. The existence of those bonds committed the railroads to the regular payment of interest at pre-agreed rates. In times of prosperity and high profits, that was not a serious problem. During periods of losses or generally poor business conditions, however, it was quite a different story. One of the greatest railroad men of the last century, the improbable Albert Fink, calculated in the 1870s that the bill for fixed costs (including interest payments) often amounted to well over half the annual operating costs for railroads. This provided a strong incentive to continue operations, even in bad times, when the roads could get traffic only by offering very low rates. Competitive pressure could thus drive rates to low levels much more easily than in industries which did not have such high constant costs.

Furthermore it made economic sense for the railroads to use as much of their capacity as possible. For example, it cost the roads only slightly more to carry, say, thirty rather than twenty-five cars on a freight train. And it was almost as costly to haul empty cars to a point where they were needed as it was to haul the same cars when they were loaded with freight. The result of this aspect of railroad economics was to encourage the roads to get as much freight as possible, and the most effective way to do that was to offer lower rates. In situations where two or more railroads competed for traffic in the same region or between the same points, the result usually was a pattern of rate wars seeking to avoid as much unused capacity as possible. The peculiar combination of high constant costs and the imperative to utilize as much capacity as was feasible meant that rates could be driven to such low points that the railroads would eventually collapse financially. Shippers might gain merrily in the short run, but as soon as one road had outlasted the others, it might use its new monopoly position to set rates at whatever levels it chose, and the shipper would be forced to pay them. These simple economic facts of life made the railroads a chaotic, unstable industry with rates that fluctuated wildly over time in a single region and that were dissimilar in different parts of the country (depending to some extent on the degree of monopoly or competition in a particular area).

Such a situation could be alleviated only by some kind of cooperation between roads or by the creation of a central body to set and enforce fair and uniform rates to satisfy both the railroaders and the public interest. The unhappy state of affairs, in other words, could be relieved only by new methods of competition.

The railroads attempted to bring order in their own house by joining together to create cartels (usually called pools or associations) whose purpose was to set rates or allocate traffic between cooperating roads (a cartel is simply a combination of independent business organizations formed to regulate production, pricing, or marketing of goods in manufacturing, or rates and traffic in transportation). These methods inevitably proved inadequate to the task. That was because all such agreements were voluntary and thus could not be enforced in courts of law, and because it was not possible to keep someone in the cartel or association from breaking the agreement by cutting rates (sometimes secretly through rebates to shippers) in an attempt to better his own position. In addition, of course, railroad cartels raised very serious political questions about the fairness and legality of businessmen conspiring to set rates by cooperation between theoretically competitive businesses.

The political response was not long in coming, and the railroads became the first major industry after the Civil War to be the target of widespread political attacks. Mercantile and shipping interests combined with agrarian groups to provide the main impetus for a series of state laws which came to be called the Granger laws after the farm organization which supported them. The purpose of that legislation was to set maximum rates and outlaw the charging of relatively higher rates for short hauls than for long ones. The latter provisions were a kind of state mercantilism designed to force the railroads to create more business in those states through lower short-haul rates. In fact, from the standpoint of costs, it *was* usually more expensive per-ton-mile for railroads to load, unload, and rearrange freight cars frequently for a group of short hauls than to route shipments on long hauls between two major rail points; as railroad historian Albro Martin has written, "no rate-making practice was more firmly rooted in the economic realities of railroad competition." But this apparent discrimination nevertheless drew much public criticism. After the Supreme Court's 1886 Wabash case ruling that only Congress could regulate interstate commerce, the state regulations aimed at remedying situations such as this were severely weakened. Pressure grew for a national law to outlaw pooling and cartels in railroading and to prohibit rate discrimination.

Additional public concern over the railroads had its origin in the unsavory financial wheeling and dealing of such railroad promoters as Jay Gould and Jim Fisk. Manipulating the prices of securities and bilking unwary speculators intent on easy money, such scoundrels weakened some roads and virtually destroyed others. These escapades inspired an early and delightful contribution to the robber baron view of the coming of big business, *Chapters of Erie* (1886) by Charles Francis Adams, Jr. and his brother Henry. "Pirates . . . are not extinct;" they lamented in a heavily punctuated passage, "they have only transferred their operations to the land, and conducted them in more or less accordance with the forms of law; until, at last, so great a proficiency have they attained, that the commerce of the world is more equally but far more heavily taxed in their behalf, than would ever have entered into their wildest hopes while, outside the law, they simply made all comers stand and deliver." Congress responded to the cries for action in 1887, passing the Interstate Commerce Act.

The federal government's regulatory role was weak for a time, but later legislation during the progressive era (including the Hepburn Act of 1906, the Mann-Elkins Act of 1910, and the Transportation Act of 1920) converted the railroads into a fully regulated industry whose rates were set by the Interstate

Commerce Commission. The peculiar competitive problems of the railways, as men like Albert Fink had known since the early 1870s, could be solved only by cartels, and the eventual political solution turned out to be one big federally administered cartel.

Although it is easy to see the desirability of control by a regulatory body that would take not only the railroad interests but also the public interest into account, it is also clear that the regulatory job done by the Interstate Commerce Commission was not a particularly good one. Albro Martin, in his *Enterprise Denied: Origins of the Decline of American Railroads, 1897–1917* (1971), for example, denounced the regulation spawned by "archaic Progressives," finding it so inept and harshly punitive that he blamed it for much of the later decline of the nation's railroads. Others would argue that the ICC was—like most regulatory commissions—dominated by the industry that was supposed to be regulated and thus unable to do an effective job. One need not, however, take such an extreme view as Martin's or that of the critics of the opposing school to see that the difficulties of resolving the competitive dilemma presented by the railroads were great and that the nation did not solve them very well. There was too much politics and not enough objective, informed regulation. Most of that story, however, belongs to the twentieth century, when railroads were unable to compete with the automobile and the trucking industry. For our purposes it is important only to acknowledge that the railroads were the first big businesses to grapple with the difficulties of high constant costs and so-called ruinous competition. Big businesses in manufacturing industries, as we will see, presented somewhat similar problems, but the difficulties were not as acute as the railroads', and the solution was somewhat different.

PRECONDITIONS FOR BIG BUSINESS

In looking at the appearance and spread of big businesses in the manufacturing sector of the economy, it is important to keep in mind that there were two fairly distinct chronological periods within the general time span covered in this book. First was the period up to about 1895, which was marked by the relatively slow, sporadic appearance of big business. Second, there came the great explosion of mergers from around 1895 to 1905. By about 1910 much of the industrial structure of the modern United States had been changed, and a great many of the giant corporations familiar to present-day Americans were established as powerful economic institutions. We will focus initially on the period of slow growth prior to the great turn-of-the-century proliferation of large-scale enterprises.

Various conditions had to be met before the modern giant corporation could arise in American manufacturing, and one of the most important was the widespread existence of the commodity the railroads were created to supply—transportation. Nationally oriented firms were a product of a national market, and that did not exist until the country had a comprehensive transport network. Thus much of the nation's energies both before and after 1860 went into the expansion and improvement of transport. Turning first to turnpikes and then to canals and finally to the railroads, Americans tied more and more of the country together with increasingly reliable and less expensive means of moving people and products. Much of the subsequent success of the national economy rested on the existence of a large domestic market which made the fruits of industrialization available, and that internal market relied on a well-developed transportation system. After the completion of New York's Erie Canal in 1825, other states followed in the construction of waterways designed to encourage economic expansion. The role of state governments in creating canals was very important, and the economic advantages of better transport were great, as such studies as Carter Goodrich (ed.), *Canals and American Economic Development* (1961) and Harry Scheiber, *Ohio Canal Era* (1969) have clearly shown. Other cities or regions selected the newer means of transportation, the railroad; cooperation between the businessmen of Baltimore and the state of Maryland, for example, resulted in that city's pathbreaking role in choosing a rail route (the B & O) rather than a canal to the interior. In a process described in encyclopedic detail in B. H. Meyer's *History of Transportation in the United States before 1860* (1917), the nation's avenues of transport grew ever more numerous and lengthy. By the end of the 1850s, over 3,000 miles of canals and 30,000 miles of railroads had been completed. Canal construction was on the wane by about 1850, but the railroad network grew very substantially until the close of the 1880s, totaling about 165,000 miles of road in operation in 1890. By the time of the explosive merger movement at the end of the century, in fact, the nation probably had more lines than it really needed as a result of duplication of facilities and expansion into some areas which did not have enough traffic to support the railways.

The importance of this transportation system to the coming of big business was considerable. Only a national market could call forth truly large, nationally oriented manufacturing corporations. So long as the transportation system remained crude and incomplete, the costs of a manufacturer's marketing his goods in distant areas were too high to encourage entry into these regions. Even if he were an efficient producer, the relatively high costs of carrying his goods over considerable distances would add so much to the final price that the goods could not compete with those of local manufacturers whose products traveled shorter distances. For example, Norman Crockett's study of *The Woolen Industry of the Midwest* (1970) demonstrated that larger, more efficient eastern mills had no hope of breaking into the midwestern market until shipping costs declined. "Transportation charges on eastern manufactures shipped to the Middle West declined steadily during the 1870s and 1880s," Crockett noted, "and in the process woolen mills in the region lost a substantial portion of their previous protection from eastern shippers." Such occurrences were repeated time and time again throughout the nineteenth century. The construction of a good nationwide transport system was, therefore, a necessary economic precondition for the rise of big business, because only such a system could create a national market.

It was perhaps also necessary from a psychological point of view. Earlier in the century, before the existence of good transportation, a manufacturer was simply not very likely to think of penetrating distant markets which could not be reached by water. Overland transport was prohibitively expensive, and it was not possible to build a nationwide manufacturing firm until that situation was altered. Only after the country "shrank" because of the transportation revolution did men find cause to dream of building far-flung manufacturing empires.

Another development crucial to the coming of big business was a "revolution" closely related to the vast changes in transportation—a "communications revolution." As the first chapter indicated, the turn-of-the-century giant enterprise engaged in a great many different kinds of highly interrelated functions over large geographical areas. This implied the ability to communicate rapidly and reliably, and early nineteenth-century businesses simply had no such capability. Communication by mail was very slow and very uncertain. Businessmen would, for example, often send two or three copies of the same letter to increase the likelihood of getting the message delivered. Improvements in the postal system could help, but the real breakthrough came with the telegraph.

In the two decades from 1846 through 1866, the telegraph industry grew from a primitive system with a few lines along the eastern seaboard to a comprehensive web of wires connecting the country. Cementing an early, mutually beneficial partnership, the telegraph and the railroad marched together across the continent. Telegraph lines were built along railroad rights-of-way, thus saving the telegraph companies high land-clearing costs. The railroads, because they were complex, large-scale enterprises, found the telegraph essential to the intricate operations of their large rail systems. Moving steadily toward a private monopoly in those two decades, the telegraph industry emerged in 1866 as virtually a single firm—Western Union. As the industry's leading historian, Robert L. Thompson, pointed out in his *Wiring a Continent* (1947), Western Union's services proved of much use to the economy. "The businessman, the banker, the broker, and the capitalist were enabled to operate upon a constantly broadening basis," Thompson commented, "as it became feasible to reach out over hundreds or even thousands of miles and obtain intelligence within a matter of minutes. The increased scope of the operations which the telegraph made possible was a significant factor in the development of big business and the rise of finance capitalism." The appearance of the telephone later in the century increased the ease of communications, but it was the telegraph which first brought the speed of electronic communications within reach of the potential empire builder.

Such economic advances as a national transportation and communications network certainly helped make big business possible, but they did not in a simple and immediate sense call it forth. Other things had to change. Businessmen had to experience other problems and opportunities before the economy produced substantial numbers of giant firms.

VERTICAL GROWTH

In the years prior to 1895, those substantial numbers of big businesses arose in two fairly distinct patterns. One was growth of a single firm via vertical integration, wherein a business would perceive a large potential market and find that to reach the market effectively, it had to engage in new functions. That is, it could not simply produce goods but had to do other things as well, such as move into the marketing of its goods. A big business usually engaged in a number of different activities, such as purchasing or growing its raw materials, fabricating those materials into goods, transporting its own products, wholesaling them, or even taking care of retailing them to consumers. A firm which did a number of different things was said to be vertically integrated because it handled the necessary activities on various rungs of the ladder reaching from raw materials all the way up to final consumers. If a company started out just as a producer of goods and then moved into marketing, it was said to integrate forward (that is, closer to the final consumer at the top of the ladder). And if it moved into owning its own raw material sources, it had integrated backward (that is, further away from the functions at the top of the ladder). Some firms grew to be big businesses by expanding vertically (usually forward into marketing) and achieving such success that they became large and powerful corporations. This pattern of becoming or creating a big business will be referred to here as "vertical growth."

The other general method by which big businesses arose was "horizontal growth." In that case, a number of producers who all did the same thing would join together to form a combination of their interests. This kind of firm was formed horizontally rather than vertically, because it was an amalgamation of firms which all engaged only in production or transportation; the newly born combination was usually not engaged in the full range of activities on the vertical rungs of the ladder. Instead it arose through a combination of similar businesses. When people spoke of "the trusts" around the turn of the century, they usually were thinking of the companies which began by this method of horizontal growth.

This general division of the rise of big business into vertical and horizontal growth oversimplifies matters. Some big businesses of the period grew through a combination of the two methods, and one could cite exceptions to the overall descriptions of the two growth processes. Nevertheless, the general interpretation of the two paths to bigness, vertical and horizontal, explains more about the rise of big business than other approaches historians have tried. Alfred D. Chandler, Jr.'s important article in the *Business History Review* (Spring 1959), "The Beginnings of 'Big Business' in American Industry," was the first study to emphasize that the vertical route to large-scale organization was of major importance. Previous historians had concentrated on the horizontal combinations, but the usefulness of Chandler's more all-inclusive framework has been widely accepted. There is still, however, substantial disagreement about the basic motivation behind the creation of big business in the first instance.

The big businesses that arose primarily through vertical growth were a mixed lot, more difficult to analyze than the horizontal combinations. Perhaps the most effective explanation of the process of vertical expansion is to say that businessmen usually began as producers and, in the course of increasing the scale of their operations, they found shortcomings in the existing mechanisms by which they obtained raw materials or sold their finished goods. Those shortcomings led them to integrate backward or forward into functions they had not performed initially. In the process of meeting a new demand more efficiently as a result of their integration, some businessmen managed to build very large firms which clearly qualified as big businesses. The companies usually grew without significant mergers, expanding to greater size primarily on the basis of vertical growth. Their success often led others to follow their lead, and it was important to be an early imitator if one couldn't be the real innovator who assembled resources in a new way. Because the successful innovations of one company quickly drew imitators, the industry usually came to be dominated by several large firms. Such an industry characterized by a few large companies is called an oligopoly, an unlovely word created by economists. Many of the nation's industries were oligopolies by 1910, and such concentration of production among a relatively small number of firms in an industry involved companies built by horizontal as well as by vertical growth.

Those who pioneered in the building of large, vertically integrated companies usually encountered problems either in marketing their goods or in acquiring their supplies. Marketing was the more important of the two problems, at least in terms of generating big businesses. The merchandising system in use before the coming of big business was one in which almost all manufactured goods except those sold to local customers were marketed through independent wholesale merchants. A web of commercial agents tied the economy together, gathering goods from a number of producers and distributing them to a diffuse market of relatively small and scattered buyers. The independent merchants also extended credit to manufacturers, arranged for the transportation of goods, and performed other services, all of which made them the wealthiest and most powerful group of businessmen in the country. They played vital roles in encouraging manufactures and in backing internal improvements in transportation and communications, as illustrated by a number of studies such as Peter Coleman's *The Transformation of Rhode Island* (1963). The merchants' control over marketing rested on the nature of products and of markets, and independent wholesalers met the needs of manufacturers very well as long as the products in which they dealt required only to be stored and shipped, without complications in transport or handling. Once products appeared which called for special handling or particular marketing expertise, however, the merchants proved less useful. Perishable goods and technologically complex goods both presented real difficulties for a marketing network geared to items which stored fairly well for long periods and which necessitated no expertise or demonstrations. Goods which called for new marketing techniques appeared in a number of industries in the last half of the nineteenth century and the early years of the twentieth. These changes in the nature of products sometimes led innovative producers to integrate forward because they could handle their own merchandising better than could the old mercantile system.

Similarly, alterations in manufacturers' needs for inputs or raw materials encouraged some firms to integrate backward toward those sources. In the antebellum economy, manufacturers had learned to live with the difficulties of procuring supplies through independent merchants. Once businesses began to produce on a larger scale, however, they often felt increasingly vulnerable because they had so little control over their supply sources. Mass production called for a steady stream of large quantities of raw materials, and the old fluctuations in supply (and consequently in the cost of inputs and final products) became less tolerable. In order to assure themselves of adequate supplies at reasonably stable costs to make for a smoother flow of materials through the production process, some manufacturers integrated backward. Makers of iron and steel, for example, bought lands with ore deposits or coal to guard against the ups and downs of the open market in iron ore or fuels. Another reason for backward integration was to achieve a more uniform quality of raw materials. The latter case was most frequent in industries which involved high levels of technology, such as steel or petroleum. Backward integration often increased the efficiency of firms and contributed to their evolution into big businesses. Shortcomings in the mechanisms for obtaining raw materials, then, like marketing problems, encouraged the coming of the modern, vertically integrated corporation. By examining in more detail the experience of several big businesses that appeared through vertical growth, we will be able to understand better this route to bigness.

One of the most striking illustrations of the coming of big business via vertical growth was the history of the meatpacking industry. In the decades before the 1870s, the industry consisted of a number of small companies which slaughtered and packed pork in the great midwestern centers of the industry, especially Chicago. Packers would cure the pork or ship it in brine over considerable distances. Beef, however, was handled differently. It did not stay fresh for very long after slaughtering, and the result was that cattle were shipped on the hoof by rail from the midwestern stockyard centers such as Omaha, Kansas City, and Chicago. The railroads built widespread facilities to handle the movement of cattle from the West to the urban centers in the East. Once the animals arrived in the East, they were slaughtered and sold by local butchers. A great opportunity awaited the man who could devise and implement a more efficient way to handle this trade.

That man turned out to be Gustavus Swift. Swift perceived (as did a few others) that if the cattle could be slaughtered and prepared in the midwestern stockyard areas and then shipped to distant markets, considerable savings could be achieved. At the western end, large numbers of animals could be systematically and efficiently butchered in large-scale slaughterhouses, which would reduce the costs of preparing the beef for market. More savings would result when the beef was shipped because only ready-to-market meat (called dressed beef) was transported, not the entire animal with all its inedible parts as well as the meat. The success of any such plans depended first on improvements in the technology of refrigeration, and Swift watched with interest the early experimental shipments of dressed beef in the 1870s. The imperfect refrigerated rail cars of those years, as Oscar Anderson's *Refrigeration in America* (1953) indicated, quickly gave way to much better, more reliable ones.

Swift, who had come to Chicago in 1875 as a buyer for a Boston meat concern, soon became convinced that with improved refrigeration he could successfully market dressed beef. In 1878 he formed a new business to attempt to implement his ideas. The concern faced a number of problems in displacing the old set of arrangements between shippers, eastern butchers, and the railroads, which had substantial investments in facilities to handle the movement of live cattle. By exploiting the competition between railroads, as the recent work of Mary Kujovich (*Business History Review,* Winter 1970) has shown, Swift was able to get his products shipped by rail to eastern cities in his own refrigerated cars. The real problem, though, lay with the distribution network.

In order to make his plans work, Swift needed not only shipping facilities but refrigerated warehouses to store the beef once it arrived. He could not simply have it unloaded on the streets of New York on a summer's day and then wait for buyers. The existing wholesale marketing arrangements for fresh meat were of no use to him, because they did not include the refrigerated facilities he required. He was thus forced to build a network of branch houses to store and sell chilled beef. During the 1880s, Swift and Company created a nationwide web of the necessary facilities, often forming partnerships with local jobbers willing to join the new venture. Once Swift overcame initial consumer resistance to meat slaughtered days before in distant places, his products found a booming market because they were as good as freshly butchered meats and were substantially cheaper.

After Swift's integration into marketing, the company quickly became a complex big business. The firm's purchases of live animals, the activities of its large slaughtering and butchering plants in the Midwest, and the transport of its dressed beef all had to be coordinated very carefully to match the fluctuating demand in the cities where the meat was consumed. Swift and Company was an early user of telegraph services to allow rapid communication between its far-flung operations. Before the merger wave of the 1890s, the firm had created a vertically integrated big business as a result of the expansion into marketing made necessary by the shortcomings of the existing distribution network.

Swift's success quickly attracted imitators anxious to cash in on the new trade. By the 1890s, men like Philip Armour had followed on Swift's heels and had carved out a share of the market by building similar, integrated businesses.

Critics soon began including the "Beef Trust" on their list of concentrated industries. The meatpackers were the target of one of the era's earliest "muckrakers," Upton Sinclair. In his novel *The Jungle* (1906), Sinclair portrayed the drudgery and hopelessness of the slaughterhouse workers and sounded a plea for socialism, dedicating his book to the workingmen of America. Most public criticism focused not on working conditions in the industry, but on the collusion of big packers. The results of a federal investigation published in 1905 (the *Report of the Commissioner of Corporations on the Beef Industry*), though, indicated relatively little illegal activity by Swift and other meatpackers. Swift's company, like those of his alert competitors such as Armour, had not evolved into a big business by absorbing or colluding with other meatpackers—instead, they had grown through internal expansion begun by integration into marketing.

Another firm that rose to national significance after integrating forward to market a perishable item was the United Fruit Company. That firm experienced its growth during the height of the merger movement at the turn of the century, but it was not created by horizontal merger. Its history closely parallels that of Swift and Company and is a good illustration of vertical growth. United Fruit grew into a major business by making a new fruit—the banana—available to consumers in the United States. Before the Civil War, the banana was not sold in American markets, but by the end of the 1860s some shipments had begun to arrive in port cities. Because of its highly perishable nature, it could not be sold in interior regions. Even after steamships were introduced in the 1870s and 1880s to speed the hauling of fruit from the Caribbean, the poor marketing facilities inland largely restricted consumption of bananas to the coastal cities. The commercial produce network in the nation's interior lacked adequate warehouses refrigerated (for summers) and heated (for winters). The innovator who followed Swift's pattern to create a national market was a Boston businessman named Andrew W. Preston.

Preston helped create the United Fruit Company in 1899, and as its first president he worked to build an integrated business which could overcome the shortcomings of the existing marketing system. The firm created a nationwide network of wholesale houses equipped with the necessary cooling and heating apparatus to allow sales in many areas. Within two years, distributing outlets were opened in twenty-one major cities, and business was booming. Within ten years of its creation, United Fruit had become one of the country's major corporations and boasted more than $40 million in assets. Although no Upton Sinclair appeared to write a novel depicting the less admirable side of its operations, United Fruit later became a symbol of United States economic imperialism, exercising great political and economic influence in what Americans sometimes condescendingly referred to as the banana republics of Latin America.

Marketing problems led others besides the purveyors of perishable goods into vertical integration. Early firms in the electrical industry, for example, created major big businesses primarily through internal expansion and vertical integration. An intelligent strategy of integration was only one of the factors which explained the success of the industry's two giants, General Electric and Westinghouse. As Harold C. Passer's *The Electrical Manufacturers, 1875–1900* (1953) argued, both mergers and and the advantage of monopoly over production facilities resulting from patent laws played a part. However, the two firms that dominated the industry by the early twentieth century could never have grown large if they had not taken the initiative in marketing to overcome the inadequacy of the antebellum marketing channels.

Though its origins lay in the preceding decade, the electrical industry emerged as a significant business in the 1880s. Thomas Edison's enterprises began in 1879 and expanded in subsequent years, producing both heavy industrial machinery to generate and transmit electrical energy and also lamps to convert the new energy source into light. The several Edison businesses were combined in 1889 to form the Edison General Electric Company, one of the two firms that joined to spawn the General Electric Company in 1892. The other firm was the Thomson-Houston Electric Company, begun in 1882. General Electric's great rival, Westinghouse, was founded in 1884 by George Westinghouse. All these early electrical manufacturers encountered very difficult problems in introducing a new product so technologically complex that the existing marketing system of independent wholesalers could not handle it. The new industry found two major kinds of markets for its products. One was the growing number of central stations that generated and transmitted electricity to a group of local customers. The other was the "isolated system," in which a factory, store, or home had its own generator and internal lighting or electrically driven machinery, rather than drawing electricity from a central station. In either case the traditional merchandising channels simply proved irrelevant to the particular needs of the manufacturers.

The merchandising difficulties sprang from the technological nature of the product. First, the products were very costly and were dangerous in the hands of people who did not understand their use and maintenance. A number of disastrous fires, injuries, and deaths marred the early years of the industry because the destructive potential of electrical energy was considerable. It would not do simply to ship equipment to a customer and hope for the best, because resulting disasters would constitute what the president of Thomson-Houston called in 1887 "a serious drawback" to the wider introduction of electricity. The only satisfactory solution was to integrate forward into marketing by creating special departments to handle the installation of the goods, to instruct the customers thoroughly in the proper operation of the apparatus, and to take care of repairing the system when necessary. Because the industry was so new, the manufacturers themselves had to take the initiative and supply a body of trained men to provide the necessary expertise and service.

The other technological difficulty lay in the particular needs of individual customers. Because the requirements of buyers were often unique (especially in cases where the electrical machinery was to be used to supply power for manufacturing), it was essential to have a well-trained force of company engineers to consult closely with potential customers. Westinghouse met this requirement by establishing, in the company's earliest days, a subsidiary engineering firm to market its products. Thomson-Houston (before it became part of GE) and Edison General Electric found it essential to supply similar services in the 1880s. By the end of that decade, the three major electrical companies had all established national marketing systems with sales offices and trained personnel who had the vital expertise to secure orders, install and operate equipment safely, and follow up with repair services.

As the history of the early electrical manufacturers shows,

in new industries with particular marketing needs, it was all but inevitable that producers would find themselves creating large, complex, vertically integrated enterprises. Their goods just didn't fit comfortably into a merchandising system composed of the old mercantile network of independent wholesalers. Expansion and the assumption of additional economic functions as a result of similar shortcomings in the old distribution network characterized firms in a number of other industries in the last half of the nineteenth century and the early years of the twentieth. Early producers of such goods as harvesters, sewing machines, heavy industrial machinery of various kinds, and new office machines such as adding machines, typewriters, and cash registers often found it necessary to supply such services as demonstrations, consumer credit, and repairs. When the automobile industry appeared after 1900, producers found that similar problems forced them to exercise some control over dealers to assure the proper introduction, sale, and repair of what was then a completely new product.

Big businesses also grew in response to shortcomings in the system for supplying raw materials. Considerable vertical integration existed, for example, in the steel industry by the early 1890s. Andrew Carnegie's steel enterprises led the way toward integration during the 1870s and 1880s, as Joseph Wall's *Andrew Carnegie* (1970) demonstrated. Carnegie marshaled capital and invested it in the latest, most technologically advanced production facilities. The dominance of his companies rested on their ability to produce at lower costs than their competitors. To achieve that position, Carnegie's enterprises operated on a large scale and engaged in considerable backward integration. Steel was made from pig iron, and Carnegie determined by the mid-1870s to control much of his own supply of that raw material. Fluctuations in the quantity, the price, and the quality of pig iron bought on the open market led the Carnegie businesses to produce their own supplies to feed their Bessemer converters, which in turn fed their rolling mills. Through the efforts of Henry Clay Frick, they soon moved even further backward, acquiring their own sources of iron ore, coal, and coke for fuel. Carnegie Steel even had its own fleet of steamships and a company railroad to transport its materials. James H. Bridge marveled in his *Inside History of the Carnegie Steel Company* (1903) that "from the moment these crude stuffs were dug out of the earth until they flowed in a stream of liquid steel in the ladles, there was never a price, profit, or royalty paid to an outsider." Because they found that they could better assure themselves of a steady, reliable flow of inputs at low prices by integrating backward, producers like Carnegie sometimes expanded into new functions in order to make themselves, as Carnegie put it, more nearly "independent of the general market." Other steelmakers soon followed Carnegie's lead and integrated backward.

As large, vertically integrated enterprises developed in the American economy, they assumed a wide range of new functions and at the same time aroused some bitter complaints about their size and power. But collusion and conspiracy do not seem to explain their success, for most grew without significant benefit of mergers or cartel behavior. In some instances, such as the cases of Swift and the electrical producers, new and better products were supplied. One may condemn, as many did, the fact that their workers did not share more of the resulting profits. One may also argue that the businessmen received a more than satisfactory reward. Nevertheless, the big businesses that arose through vertical growth appeared to owe their success primarily to just the sort of creativity and cost-consciousness that Americans professed to admire in their economic system. That is, however, considerably less true of many of the big businesses created through horizontal growth.

HORIZONTAL GROWTH

The successful businesses that had their origins in horizontal mergers before 1895 usually went through a roughly common set of experiences. First, a number of manufacturers would enter an industry (often a new industry), producing goods in volume in factories which were sometimes quite costly. For a time, all would be well; profits would be comfortable and the businesses would expand. As the market began to fill up, however, producers found that they had to compete vigorously to keep or enlarge their share of the market. Most manufacturers tried to do so by cutting the prices on their goods. After a period of price competition (usually described as "ruinous" or "destructive" by the businessmen), they would find that profits and prices were not meeting their expectations and would begin to search for a solution.

Since businessmen, like human beings in general, are prone to look for solutions that require the least possible change from their previous situations, they first looked for a way out that would allow them to remain separate, independent businesses. The basic problem they were trying to overcome was the difficulty of regulating production levels and prices in order to assure steady profits, as noted by many studies then and later, such as the essays in William Z. Ripley's *Trusts, Pools and Corporations* (1905). If everyone would just behave properly, restricting his output and maintaining his prices, the days of comfortable profits might be regained. So, like the railroads before them, manufacturers turned to the cartel, a loose form of organizational control which seemed to hold out the promise of halting the overproduction and falling prices while at the same time allowing each producer to remain an independent businessman. The cartel might take a number of forms, but the most common was the trade association. Producers of, say, steel rails could join together to form a Steel Rail Association to provide a convenient format in which they might agree to fix prices, set output quotas, or divide the market in some manner.

From the point of view of the businessmen involved, there were two things wrong with the cartel or trade association solution. One was that such arrangements drew political lightning like iron rods in a thunderstorm. After the Sherman Act became law in 1890 as a result of that political reaction, cartels were of very questionable legality. Perhaps a more important shortcoming was that the associations did not work. Although they tried various ways to enforce the decisions of the cartels, producers ultimately found that there was no effective way to do so. A few producers almost always stayed out, undermining the cartels. Furthermore, the agreements were always voluntary and could not be enforced in courts of law because they were not legal contracts. They could have worked only if the participants had strictly lived up to the terms set by the associations. But the temptation to cut prices and attempt to conceal that fact by paying secret rebates to wholesalers or other customers was too strong. Any downward fluctuation in business conditions was almost certain to flush out at least one greedy or failing manufacturer who wanted more profits than the pool had allotted him. Another problem was that any pool or cartel that was successful even for a brief time quickly lured new producers into the industry, which shortly brought prices and profits down again. The associations were, in the terse and contemptuous judgment of John D. Rockefeller, "ropes of sand."

Usually the next step after the failure of cartels was horizontal combination, in which all or many of the major producers in an industry would form a single firm, at least in the legal sense. The first form in which this occurred was the trust, pioneered in 1882 by Rockefeller's Standard Oil. In that form of organization, a group of trustees (leading producers in the industry) received the common stock of different corporations in exchange for trust certificates, thereby effecting legal control by the trust over the properties of the participating firms. This legal device attempted to get around the common law prohibition against one corporation's holding stock in another without explicit statutory authority. After 1889, it was possible to form a horizontal combination by incorporating in New Jersey, which enacted a general incorporation law permitting corporations chartered there to own stock in other such businesses. This resulted in more and more combinations being put together as holding companies rather than trusts—a slight legal distinction which the public ignored. The popularity of the word "trust" resulted in its also being used to denote holding companies, as well as looser business alliances such as pools and associations. By achieving the legal status of trusts or holding companies, the combinations were in a stronger position to control the price and output of their constituent parts.

Once the leading producers had formed a combine, the new corporation often functioned for a time as a loose amalgam of divisions which retained much of their former autonomy. This situation really amounted to a continuation of cartel behavior, because the firm's new central office exercised little effective control and direction other than acting as a general forum in which price and output decisions were reached. If all went well for the combination and the profits turned out as expected, this loose kind of corporation might continue for a time. However, if trouble appeared in the form of competition from old "outside" producers who had refused to give up their independence by joining the combination, or from new competitors (sometimes foreign concerns), the combination usually was forced to take away the autonomy of its subdivisions and exercise more unified control from the central office. Often, the most effective way to maintain market position and profits was to become more competitive by ordering the closing of the less efficient plants, and by integration forward or backward to perform marketing functions more cheaply or obtain raw materials more inexpensively. In that way, many of the firms which started as loose, almost cartel-like horizontal combinations evolved into vertically integrated, centrally administered businesses. Some remained loose combinations for many years, and others collapsed and disappeared from the roll of American corporations. Most of the successful combinations, however, did become vertically integrated, modern big businesses. The general horizontal growth pattern just described was the road taken by a number of large-scale enterprises created before 1895, and it was the route traveled by the majority of the giant corporations built in the years after 1895, in the most explosive phase of the merger movement.

The behavior of prices was important in the process outlined above, and the general movement in price levels in the long stretch from the end of the Civil War to around 1895 should be kept in mind. Although the published material on prices is far from perfect, a number of scholars have compiled useful data. The most widely used price series was done by G. F. Warren and F. A. Pearson, appearing in their short monograph *Wholesale Prices for 213 Years: 1720–1932* (1932) and in their book called *Prices* (1933), both based largely on data for New York City. Those studies and others demonstrated a broad, fairly steady decline in prices from the end of the Civil War to the mid-1890s. The wholesale price index for all commodities in 1866 (according to the Warren and Pearson studies) stood at 174; by 1870 it was down to 135, by 1880 to 100, and by 1890 to 82. Of course the pattern of declining prices was not continuous; in some years prices did increase. The overall thirty-year pattern, however, was definitely one of falling prices. The wholesale costs of every major category of goods—farm products, food, leather, textiles, fuels, metals, building materials, drugs and chemicals, household goods, and distilled spirits—fell considerably during the years which produced big business. When manufacturers complained bitterly about plummeting prices and declining profits, it is clear that they were at least correct about prices.

To a considerable extent, the falling prices were a reflection of declining costs of production brought on by the spread of mass production techniques and important technological improvements. Before about 1870, as Lance Davis and Douglass North pointed out in their *Institutional Change and American Economic Growth* (1971), most industries were subject to what economists call "constant returns to scale," which simply means that while a bigger factory would allow the production of more goods, the costs per unit of output were about the same for large as for small producers. In many important industries after the Civil War, however, technological changes brought "economies of scale," which meant that a large, expensive plant could produce goods more cheaply on a per-unit basis than could a smaller one, so long as the larger plant operated at high levels of output. The Bessemer process of steelmaking, for example, brought economies of scale to big producers in that industry. Other examples included petroleum refining and flour milling. Since such industries almost always saw the growth of very capital-intensive production, the firms involved experienced high fixed costs somewhat similar to those earlier encountered on the railroads. Economies of scale, coupled with the existence of competitive conditions in many industries, brought reduced prices. Firms in such industries found that their high fixed costs and economies of scale meant that success lay in keeping the production processes running "full and steady" to keep their costs per unit of output down. During bad times, they were willing to cut prices. As Andrew Carnegie declared during one economic downturn, "The policy today is what it has always been in poor seasons; 'scoop the market,' prices secondary; work to keep our mills running [is] the essential thing." The result of this sort of policy was, of course, more declines in prices.

The cumulative psychological impact of this long price decline on producers may readily be imagined. During the six decades before the Civil War, prices had not behaved in such a manner. Falling prices had occurred, of course, but never so relentlessly for such a long time. This steady downward trend in the prices received for manufactured goods disturbed and unnerved businessmen. It was doubtless an important element in encouraging them to turn more and more toward cooperation rather than competition and helps explain the widespread tendency in almost every branch of manufacturing to search for ways to control output and prices.

In many industries, especially new ones or ones that enjoyed some kind of significant improvements in the technology of production, manufacturers initially found themselves in an enviable position. Growth was rapid and profits were good as the producers expanded to meet the demand for their product. Eventually, however, demand leveled off as the manufacturers grew to the point where they turned out every year at least as much as (and often more than) the market wanted. Then problems set in as manufacturers struggled for a larger share of what had become an increasingly stable market. Profits might actually decline during such a period, or they might stop growing at the previously high levels. In either case, manufacturers were likely to believe themselves in trouble and to start searching for a solution.

A brief look at one minor industry, the manufacture of wire nails, will help to illustrate the above pattern. Until the 1880s, almost all nails used in America were cut nails made from metal plates. By that decade, however, a number of new competitors making nails from wire had appeared and gained ground rapidly, with production levels rising steeply. By the middle of the 1890s, the wire product had almost replaced the old cut one in the nail market. The result was that the early growth and profits in wire nails were leveling off, and producers began to find their situation less satisfactory than before. Recalling the years prior to 1895, one analyst of the industry wrote in 1897 that the "manufacturers had been fairly contented, making the comfortable profits of a new and rapidly growing business." When the pace of profit growth declined, however, the producers "cried out with one voice that they were ruined by competition." Setting aside the question of whether absolute profits really fell much or not, it is clear that the manufacturers found their new situation less pleasing than their old one. The result of manufacturers' initiatives was not a genuine trust or combination, but a cartel in the form of an association of independent wire nail makers to set pooling agreements to fix prices and output. For a short time after the cartel arrangement began, prices did rise. But soon new producers came in to take advantage of what looked like a good thing, and the pool collapsed. The experience of makers of wire nails was typical of many other industries after the Civil War.

To some extent, it may be argued that almost all industries that relied on factory or mass production went through something like the above pattern. In the cotton textile industry, the nation's first factory-dominated branch of manufacturing, the earliest attempts at forming trade organizations came in the 1850s, a time of declining profits. Because the factory did not come to many other industries until the mid-1840s or 1850s, one might anticipate that the period of good, growing profits in those industries would have lasted, say, until the early 1860s. By that time, however, the Civil War had come along and touched off a business boom, thus prolonging the era of satisfactory profits. By the early 1870s, however, the delayed pressure finally arrived, and that decade witnessed the first widespread attempts by manufacturers to form pools and cartels. This is obviously an extremely broad generalization, but it is very helpful in answering the question of why manufacturers in many industries began turning to cooperation at the particular time they did. The search for reliable methods of controlling prices and output and thereby gaining more control over profits continued until the end of the century, and it was especially common in new industries or in ones that underwent significant technological changes. The profits made by manufacturers in that period are, of course, not known except for a handful of companies. It is therefore difficult to know how accurately the picture of an initial period of expansion followed by a leveling off of growth fits the reality of the decades after Lee's surrender at Appomattox. Nevertheless there is much circumstantial evidence to suggest that it is a good explanation.

During the three decades after 1865, manufacturers in industry after industry found their profits or growth rates unsatisfactory and turned to various forms of cartel behavior for an answer. Sometimes that behavior took the form of a simple, informal pool for higher prices or lower production levels. Sometimes it manifested itself in a trade association, a somewhat more formal means of cooperation, yet one which still left each firm an independent entity. Sometimes (after the formation of Standard Oil in 1882), it went so far as a real trust or holding company which brought the surrender of autonomy by previously competing companies. In the public mind at the time, all such attempts at cooperation were "trusts;" a catchall word for any apparent concentration of economic power. As we have seen, however, only the real trust or holding company led to the modern kind of firm which constituted big business in the early years of the twentieth century.

Unfortunately very little work has been done by scholars on the looser forms of cooperation such as pools and trade associations. The recent study by Louis Galambos, *Competition & Cooperation: The Emergence of a National Trade Association* (1966) is a comprehensive look at associations in the cotton textile industry and indicates the persistence of attempts by manufacturers to gain more control over profits and output. It is clear that those loose efforts toward cooperation came in a great many industries. In looking at the manufacture of hardware, for example, William Becker (*Business History Review,* Summer 1971) found more than forty producers' trade associations in the 1870s and 1880s in the various subdivisions of that one industry. Among the industries which between 1865 and 1895 definitely engaged in some form of cartel behavior (a pool, trade association, or formal combination into a trust or holding company) are the following: textiles, iron and steel, nonferrous metals, hardware, petroleum, sugar manufacturing, tobacco manufacturing, lumber, anthracite coal, salt, leather products, cottonseed oil, liquor, glass, paper, gunpowder, and many more. The attempts at cooperation often began on a state or regional level and then later expanded to a national scale. Once businesses in a number of industries began to try cartel behavior, others began to consider it and to try it out as a means of improving their economic position. This phenomenon of imitation also appeared in the great combination movement after 1895, as we will soon see. In the 1880s and early 1890s, however, relatively few industries produced real trusts or holding companies, and even fewer of those turned out to be lasting, successful firms which became vertically integrated, complex big businesses. We will examine three of the most important industries in which cartel behavior did result in a trust or a holding company before 1895 to see in more detail how the process worked. The three combinations we will look at—in oil, sugar, and tobacco—played extremely important roles in creating and publicizing the apparently profitable road manufacturers might travel if they could form a major trust or holding company. The success of these three companies (and a few others) before 1895 paved the way for the flood of mergers after that date by fostering a widespread thirst to build combinations, a thirst satisfied in the turn-of-the-century merger movement.

The pioneer enterprise in the story of industrial combinations was, of course, Standard Oil. The importance of the rise of that firm was succinctly summarized by Ida Tarbell in her *History of the Standard Oil Company* (1925): "It was the first in the field, and it has furnished the methods, the charter, and the traditions for its followers." Standard was the first great horizontal combination in manufacturing, and no other company has been the subject of so many historical inquiries. Henry Demarest Lloyd's passionate *Wealth Against Commonwealth* (1894) set the tone for most of the subsequent highly critical interpretations. Of the relatively recent studies, the two most detailed (and largely sympathetic) works are Ralph and Muriel Hidy, *Pioneering in Big Business, 1882–1911* (1955) and Harold F. Williamson, Arnold R. Daum, and others, *The American Petroleum Industry: The Age of Illumination, 1859–1899* (1959). The evolution of Standard Oil, as all its historians have demonstrated, was a protracted struggle by John Rockefeller and his colleagues to bring order and stability to an unruly industry by imposing centralized control and reaping enormous profits as a result.

In the early years of the industry, after Edwin Drake drilled the nation's first oil well in Titusville, Pennsylvania (1859), large numbers of businessmen rushed into the new industry. Production costs were relatively low (though they later rose as refining technology improved), and soon numerous firms were competing intensely. Prices and the supply of crude oil and its refined forms fluctuated wildly. Three refining centers quickly arose—Pittsburgh, Philadelphia, and Cleveland, and from the Ohio refiners came the man who eventually managed to organize the industry, John Davison Rockefeller.

The future oil magnate started out in 1859 in the produce commission business and entered petroleum refining in 1863. From the very first, Rockefeller showed a keen ability to choose able associates, and he began gathering around him the nucleus of a talented group of financial and managerial partners. The Standard Oil Company was founded in 1867. By 1870 the firm had two large, efficient refineries which represented about a tenth of the nation's refining capacity. Because his company was Cleveland's largest, Rockefeller was able to secure preferential rates from railroads anxious to haul his large, steady shipments. He persuaded other Cleveland refiners to join with him to secure lower rates and better profits. Arguing that the other Cleveland firms could not compete with Standard's efficiency and lower rail rates, Rockefeller pressured them to sell out to him or face ruin. By about 1871 Standard Oil dominated the petroleum business in Cleveland and was turning its attention to national developments.

Refiners all over the country were growing unhappy with the continuing unsettled state of the industry. Manufacturers were turning out kerosene and other products in such volume that prevailing profits and prices seemed threatened by over-capacity. In order to improve their own economic position, re-finers needed to achieve some degree of control over the produc-tion of crude oil, its refining, and its transportation. Their initial answer was an attempt at a cartel, the National Refiners' Asso-ciation, begun in 1872 with Rockefeller as president. The cartel included representatives from the major refining areas (Cleve-land, Pittsburgh, New York, Philadelphia, and the crude oil regions in western Pennsylvania). Those representatives allo-cated quotas for the purchase of crude and the sale of refined oil. The firms producing crude oil quickly formed a similar cartel to regulate their end of the business. It soon became ap-parent, however, that the cartels would not work; businessmen outside the association refused to cooperate, and the agreements of the cartels were broken by their own members anxious to get more than their allotted share of the business. The cartels collapsed, doomed by their weak controls and lack of enforcement powers.

Having tried cartels and found them wanting, Rockefeller and his associates set out to build a single company to control the industry. Using the old Cleveland strategy of combining superior productive efficiency with rebates in transportation, Standard strengthened its position. Gradually, major refiners around the country were persuaded to sell out to Standard. Because they received generous rewards for their businesses in the form of stock in Standard, and because they could have a voice in the management of the combination, refiners sold out in the belief that profits could be assured by that company. These mergers were kept secret, and the various companies continued to operate under their old names. By the end of the 1870s, a great horizontal combination had been built; the Standard Oil interests controlled about nine-tenths of the nation's petroleum refining capacity.

The great horizontal amalgam, however, was an administrative and legal mess. Because the law forbade one corporation from owning stock in another and discouraged a firm chartered in one state from owning property in another state, Standard was put together with a patchwork of subterfuges. Rockefeller and his compatriots personally held the stock of the companies controlled by Standard as trustees for its stockholders in an attempt to get around the law. By 1879 an informal version of the trust had been invented by Standard: several trustees held the stock of out-of-state companies "in trust" for Standard's stockholders. Early in 1882 the arrangement was formalized by a Trust Agreement, and trust certificates were exchanged for the stock of Standard Oil. This apparently legal detour around existing laws was imitated in the 1880s by various combinations, including the trusts in sugar and distilling. Growing political pressure and the appearance of New Jersey's 1889 general incorporation law permitting one corporation to own stock in another made the trust form shortlived. It was replaced by the holding company (after 1889) as the favorite instrument for combination.

In the years after 1882, Standard Oil faced challenges from both foreign and domestic competition, challenges which led it to move to consolidate its central control over the companies it owned. In 1884 the trust opened headquarters on Broadway, from which it directed the increasing integration and expansion of its oil empire. Most of Standard's market lay overseas, and the development of Russian oil by the powerful Nobel interests led to Standard's closing inefficient refineries and relocating refining in areas closer to water transportation to cut costs and rebuff the threat from Europe. The discovery of new oil fields in the United States and the continual appearance of independent refiners led Standard to integrate backward into the production of crude oil and forward into transportation and marketing. Utilizing its efficiency, its financial strength, and the harsh techniques associated with its name—rebates, intimidation, an espionage network to report on uncooperative businessmen, and ruthless vengeance for troublemakers—Standard completed by the early 1890s a vast, vertically integrated company involved in every aspect of the petroleum business. Standard's near-monopoly position declined thereafter with the rise of competitors in the giant new oil fields in the Southwest around the turn of the century, and the Supreme Court's 1911 dissolution of Standard into a number of firms later completed the industry's transition into a business dominated by a relatively few firms rather than a single company.

Nevertheless, manufacturers in other industries learned with interest of the innovations of Standard Oil, and soon additional producers were trying to imitate its success in achieving control and bringing stability and handsome profits. Participants in the sugar refining industry were definitely interested, for their business was remarkably similar to oil refining. In the years shortly before the Civil War, major technological improvements in sugar refining, in the words of Alfred Eichner (*Emergence of*

Oligopoly: Sugar Refining as a Case Study [1969]), "had, in effect, created an entirely new industry." Those advances made it possible to mass produce for the first time sugar of uniform quality in large refineries. A number of new firms arose, built refineries with the latest technology in east coast cities, and successfully competed with the older Louisiana sugar companies. The period of the Civil War and the years immediately following it constituted good times for the manufacturers supplying the demand of urban areas in the eastern United States. During that initial period of growth, producers made "high profits" which attracted new firms and encouraged existing manufacturers to expand, according to Eichner's study.

By the 1870s, however, the industry ran into the troubles that afflicted some others in the same period—instability, falling prices, and declining profit rates due to the creation of a potential supply greater than the demand. As the initial period of growth and high profits gave way to the severe price competition of the 1870s and early 1880s, the refiners' margin of profits grew thinner and thinner. Because the industry was one that required large fixed investments, most firms soon were "no longer able to cover their full costs, if an adequate return on invested capital is included as part of these costs," Eichner reported. Investment in a sugar refinery was "sunk" into the plant and was difficult to liquidate, so even marginal producers stayed in the industry, adding to the problem of overproduction. Sugar refiners, like other manufacturers, soon turned to associations or cartels in an attempt to regulate output and prices and thus restore high profits. The first counterpart to oil's National Refiners' Association was inaugurated in sugar in 1880. Despite elaborate pooling arrangements, the cartel soon collapsed, and for the usual reasons; other attempts at cartel control followed, and they also failed. As a result, producers began to look toward combination.

After difficult negotiations, most of the big refiners reached agreement to form a horizontal combination, using the legal device Standard Oil had pioneered—the trust. In 1887 eighteen refiners joined together secretly and promulgated a trust agreement, exchanging the stock of their individual enterprises for the trust certificates. As in the case of oil mergers, producers were offered stock worth more than they had thought their businesses were worth, and they agreed to join. Soon the sugar trust found itself exercising more and more central direction over the (initially) highly autonomous subdivisions, ordering the closing of older, less efficient plants to cut costs and raise profits. In 1891 the company took advantage of the New Jersey incorporation law and reorganized itself as American Sugar Refining, a holding company.

In subsequent years, however, the sugar combine found it ever more difficult to maintain its early near-monopoly position. A new raw material source—sugar beets—arose to compete with sugarcane, and the company expended enormous financial resources to counter that threat in the 1890s. In addition, it proved impossible to keep at least a few other competitors out, despite the firm's resort to unsavory methods of competition. Those unfair practices included railroad rebates (by then definitely illegal) and attempts to strong-arm wholesalers into refusing to handle the products of any company other than American Sugar Refining. Such ruthless competition, coupled with the firm's traditional secrecy and the refusal of the company's officials to cooperate with governmental inquiries, gave the combination a bad reputation and eventually led to an (unsuccessful) antitrust suit against the corporation. Nevertheless, sugar refining had by the early 1900s evolved into an industry dominated by a few large firms and not by a single combine. As other businessmen later discovered, it often proved quite possible to control prices when the industry was composed of a relatively few big producers. The creation of the sugar combination and the subsequent success of sugar refiners in restoring profits added further luster to the appeal of horizontal combinations in the eyes of other manufacturers.

The rise of the third of the major corporations we are looking at in detail—American Tobacco—revealed a pattern strikingly similar to the one in oil and sugar. American Tobacco appeared in the cigarette industry, a new business (like petroleum and sugar). The industry arose after the Civil War and experienced very high growth rates throughout the 1870s and the first half of the 1880s. During that period, profits were good and producers were happy. By about the mid-1880s, however, demand was leveling off, and the industry entered a period of stringent competition brought on by overcapacity. The invention and use of cigarette-making machines (pioneered by James B. Duke) in the middle of that decade replaced the existing system of production by hand rollers. Mechanization of the production process immediately expanded the potential supply to great heights.

Once demand leveled off and overcapacity set in, the producers fell to intensive competition. Heavy advertising was used as a competitive weapon, and by the end of the 1880s, advertising costs had risen to approximately twenty percent of the companies' incomes. The manufacturers soon tired of the rigorous competition and began to search for stability to make profits more secure.

A few efforts at cartel behavior followed, but with little result. During the discussions among the major producers about how to resolve the problem of overcapacity and costly competition, the alternative of a cartel with pooling arrangements was considered but was rejected. The cigarette manufacturers did not really make an effort to try a formal association or cartel because they were convinced that it was too weak a form of cooperation to get the job done. The earlier experiments with cartels in the railroads, in oil, in sugar, and in other industries had clearly given that mode of seeking control a bad reputation among businessmen. Accordingly, the cigarette makers decided after months of negotiations to create a horizontal combination.

The American Tobacco Company was founded in 1890, and it was the first major combination formed as a holding company under New Jersey's freshly passed general incorporation law. As did so many other combinations, American Tobacco initially operated with highly autonomous subdivisions, but soon was centralizing control from its Manhattan headquarters and engaging in vertical integration. During the next ten or twelve years, the cigarette combination extended its influence into other branches of the tobacco manufacturing industry. Utilizing brutal competitive methods such as selective price wars to drive competitors out of business, an espionage system to monitor the activities of wholesalers, coercive agreements with jobbers to force them to handle only American Tobacco's goods, as well as the weapon of massive advertising, the tobacco combine achieved control over the manufacture of smoking tobacco, chewing tobacco, and snuff in addition to its control of cigarettes. If ever there was a "bad trust," American Tobacco qualified. The federal government finally prosecuted the firm under the Sherman Act in 1907, and the Supreme Court in 1911 upheld its conviction and ordered its breakup into several companies. Even the firms created by the dissolution of the trust were each of substantial size, however, and oligopoly proved to be almost as profitable and stable as the monopoly that American Tobacco had attempted to create. The efforts by manufacturers to control prices and avoid competition had ultimately led to a highly concentrated industry dominated by a few firms— the pattern common among numerous industries after the rise of big business.

The motivation of the men who formed these horizontal combinations was clearly somewhat different from that of the creators of giant businesses through vertical growth. Here the primary goal was to gain control over an industry in order to influence output, prices, and profits. Other purposes were, of course, involved, such as securing economies of scale and reducing costs, but the overriding objective was control over output and prices. If that goal could be reached and maintained over the long run, monopoly profits could be extracted from society. These early horizontal combinations posed a troubling question that was to grow more pressing as businessmen in other industries attempted to follow the lead of Standard Oil, American Sugar Refining, and American Tobacco—could market forces or political intervention assure that the social benefits of such combinations would equal or outweigh the costs? The economy was on the brink of a tidal wave of combinations which would make that question more important than ever.

THE GREAT MERGER WAVE

By the mid-1890s, the appearance and notoriety of various horizontal combinations in the form of trusts or holding companies had helped prepare the way for the rapid spread of such businesses. Once a few successful and widely publicized combinations had gotten underway, businessmen in many industries began to consider the possibility of duplicating in their own industries the pattern of Standard Oil, American Sugar Refining, and American Tobacco. In any sort of sudden, massive alteration in the organization of many businesses, the force of example is strong, and the new forms are "in the air" or faddish. The proliferation of conglomerates in the 1960s, for example, may be explained in large part by the fact that they became suddenly fashionable. Before a major consolidation movement could occur in the 1890s, it was essential for businessmen to have some successful examples before them. By the mid-1890s combination was "in the air." Even producers who were not necessarily unhappy with their situations found themselves thinking of mergers, as did some manufacturers in industries where it proved impossible to gain and maintain control by creating large, horizontal combinations.

In addition to the growing force of example, a number of other factors must be considered in explaining why the nation's industries turned in such a massive way to mergers just before the turn of the century. Changes in the legal environment seem to have played a contributing role in readying the economy for the rapid spread of horizontal mergers. One important development was the appearance of state general incorporation laws (such as New Jersey's in 1889) which allowed one corporation to hold stock in others, thus permitting the easy creation of holding companies. Before the advent of such legislation, it was necessary to obtain special laws from state legislatures to allow that practice, and in the general political climate of the times, that might have proved difficult. The new general incorporation laws, designed to attract industry to the states, meant that a company could obtain a charter simply by filling out a form and paying a fee, and a holding company could then operate in several states without difficulty. These legal changes were only contributors to, not causes of, the rapid spread of mergers, as Donald Dewey argued in his *Monopoly in Economics and Law* (1959).

Probably of more importance was the role of the Sherman Antitrust Act of 1890 and its interpretation by the courts. One of the interesting things about human activities is the extent to which carefully laid plans produce unintended consequences, and the political opposition to the spread of big business is such an instance. Congress had responded to public pressure to "do something" about the problem of concentration in industry by passing the Sherman Act, a very vague law which simply outlawed "every . . . combination . . . in restraint of trade." The intent of the act and of most of its supporters was to halt the spread of big businesses and to encourage a return to a more competitive economy of smaller producers. The particular way in which the law was interpreted by the courts, however, actually appears to have speeded the appearance of the modern, integrated corporation in the U.S. This was so because the courts ruled that cartel behavior was illegal under the act, but that unified combinations were in most instances acceptable. That is, the law forbade collusion by independent firms but did not necessarily outlaw the activities of holding companies created by the legal union of previously separate businesses. The result was that independent businessmen were led from cartels to combinations (holding companies) in part by the legal changes originally designed to prevent the rise of more big businesses.

As William Letwin's *Law and Economic Policy: The Evolution of the Sherman Antitrust Act* (1965) has shown, the legal thickets surrounding the place of cartel behavior and horizontal combinations in American law both before and after the

Sherman Act were dark and dense indeed. However, it is clear that American law treated such issues very differently than did the legal systems of other industrial nations. The American legal system inherited from English law a strong distaste for cartels. Although cartel behavior was increasingly tolerated in England by about the middle of the nineteenth century, it continued to be frowned upon in the United States. Furthermore, in continental European countries such as France and Germany, cartels abounded and were quite legal. Agreements reached by European cartels could be enforced in the courts, and therefore the agreements worked much more satisfactorily there than in this country. The long-term result was that small, family firms survived much longer in those countries than in America because cartels proved a legal, practical way to regulate output, markets, and prices in Europe. Since there was no legal or political pressure to move from cartel behavior to some other form of industrial organization in Europe, cartels and independent, family firms continued to flourish there well into the twentieth century.

The situation in the United States was quite different. As Hans B. Thorelli pointed out in his *The Federal Antitrust Policy* (1955), both federal and state law appeared to oppose collusive practices in restraint of trade. Because they were forbidden to engage in cartel behavior, and, more important, because cartel agreements could not be enforced in the courts, American businessmen moved more quickly to the genuine formal amalgamation of their independent companies.

The Congress placed an extremely heavy burden on the courts when it elected to pass very general, vague legislation about concentration. The Supreme Court and lesser federal courts struggled with the endless questions that arose about big business and the antitrust law. A price-fixing agreement was obviously illegal, but what were the justices to do when one company legally sold its assets to another? Were such sales illegal if they resulted in restraint of trade? How should the effort to create a monopoly be defined? What exactly was a monopoly —100 percent of an industry? 75 percent? 50 percent—or did that differ with the particular conditions in each industry? If a monopoly existed, how could it be broken up? While the courts wrestled with such dizzying puzzles, businessmen continued to organize their combinations. If the courts meant to shear the cartel sheep and bypass the integrated-firm goats, it was clearly better to be a goat than a sheep, or at least to look like one. Like the changes in state general incorporation laws, the importance of the Sherman Act was to encourage still further the growing sentiment to try horizontal combinations.

Some scholars have pointed to factors other than the legal environment to explain the big merger wave after 1895. Economist Joe S. Bain, in a contribution to Harold F. Williamson (ed.), *The Growth of the American Economy* (1944), emphasized the importance of the continued growth of the railway system in bringing about vigorous price competition which in turn touched off the merger movement. It is difficult, however, to tie the railroad closely to the huge merger wave of the turn of the century. Ralph Nelson, in his *Merger Movements in American Industry, 1895–1956* (1959), concluded after a careful review of the evidence that there was little causal connection between the additional growth of railroads after about 1880 and the merger wave after 1895. Certainly the creation of a national market and a nationwide transportation system was a necessary precondition of the explosion of horizontal combinations in the decade from 1895 to 1905, but it is difficult to explain the timing of that flurry of combinations by reference to transportation. It seems clear that a national market had been created at least fifteen years before 1895, and the nation's major cities were already linked by railroads as early as 1860. The great combination movement could surely not have happened without the prior creation of a national transport system, but it seems to have lagged somewhat behind that system.

A far more important event in unleashing the merger proliferation seems to have been the changes in the nation's capital markets. Advances in transportation and communications had made the modern, large-scale, integrated corporation a possibility. The behavior of prices, profits, and growth rates had started businessmen on a long search for cooperative means of controlling their economic environment, and pools and trade associations had proved unsatisfactory. Changes in the legal setting at the end of the 1880s had encouraged and facilitated the transition from cartels to the unified firm, and the success of a number of very well publicized horizontal combinations had led others in business to think of the possibility of creating similar organizations. Changes in the nation's capital markets provided the last impetus needed to launch the country into the great merger movement.

Before the 1890s, there was virtually no national market for industrial securities. Except for a few companies, it was not possible for potential investors to buy stocks of industrial firms as they so commonly do now. Railroad stocks and bonds accounted for almost all the securities of private businesses available to people with surplus capital in an open market. Industrial stocks were generally considered too risky for this sort of trading, though there was some small-scale trading of local industrial shares (such as in textile companies) on local markets before 1890. There was, however, no national market for industrials. As a result, owners of manufacturing businesses found their capital sunk in their firms and had little opportunity to liquidate their ownership if they cared to. For example, if a businessman owned a half-interest in a steel mill and wanted to retire, the number of people he might have sold to would have been limited to those persons with a large chunk of cash and a desire to go into the steel business. Under those circumstances he would possibly have had to stay in business for lack of a buyer or else have had to settle for less than his interest was really worth in order to attract a buyer. If, on the other hand, he owned 2,500 of the 5,000 shares in the mill and there were a large, established trade in industrial securities, he could sell all or part of his interest much more easily and probably at a better price. If there were a securities market, a large number of people could bid for small blocks of the shares and view them simply as investments and not as any real obligation to get into the steel business. Such a market would be a much more accurate and efficient mechanism for evaluating the worth of assets and turning them into cash. During the 1890s such a market arose for the first time, as the securities of industrial corporations gained widespread acceptance among investors and came to be listed on the New York Stock Exchange and traded all over the country. The creation of an industrial securities market made it very much easier to build large combinations, and the appearance of more and more successful big businesses helped expand the market for "industrials," as they were called.

Several factors had combined to produce a large pool of potential capital to underwrite the great merger wave, as Vincent Carosso pointed out in his *Investment Banking in America*. In the three decades after 1870, the flow of foreign investment into the U.S. grew ever larger, expanding from about $1.4 billion in 1870 to $3.36 billion in 1900, though most of the funds were invested in railroads. On the domestic scene, available funds from personal savings were greater than ever before. Raymond Goldsmith's *A Study of Savings in the United States* (1955–1956) indicated that the rate of growth of such savings "was at a peak in the 1870's and 1880's," thus creating a pool of capital to power the stock market growth in the 1890s. In addition, the great expansion of the railroads (since the 1850s the favorite of investors) was nearing a close, and therefore that industry began to call for less capital than previously. All these developments provided plenty of money for investment in industrial securities.

The growing attempts by businessmen to form horizontal combinations produced a ready demand for the funds investors had handy. By the end of the 1880s, a small number of the trust certificates of major horizontal combines had begun to find a market, but only among very speculative investors. Conservative investors would not think of buying any such securities because they were considered unsafe and for that reason were not listed on the New York exchange. By the early 1890s, however, this situation was changing.

During the first years of that decade, as Thomas Navin and Marian Sears have shown (*Business History Review,* June 1955), some of the new, large, and apparently legal holding companies began to issue preferred stock, sometimes with the aid of reputable bankers. These securities, aided considerably by the growing feeling that the holding companies were on sounder legal ground than the cartel-like trusts, finally found places on the nation's most important stock exchange. Many leading investment bankers, including the conservative and very prestigious J. P. Morgan, continued to regard the new industrials with mistrust, though Morgan did help finance one such company— General Electric—in 1893. When the stock market suffered a long downturn in the depression that began in that same year, however, the industrials weathered the storm better than the stocks of most railroads. By the time the economy turned up again in a few years, bankers and investors had gained considerable confidence in industrial securities. The capital markets were at last ready to receive large issues of securities from big businesses in manufacturing. When the most gilt-edged banking house of all, J. P. Morgan and Company, underwrote the creation of the Federal Steel Company in 1898, it was clear to even the most cautious of investors in this country and in Europe that it was time to get in on a good thing.

The fact that a solid, brisk market was appearing for industrial securities made it much easier for businessmen to create large combinations. It was considerably less difficult to talk independent manufacturers into giving up their companies to form part of a giant corporation if they could easily turn their shares into cash in the stock market. In addition, most bankers and promoters who helped work out the financial arrangements by which companies merged saw to it that the new combinations were capitalized at considerably more than the worth of their separate parts (this was the activity known as "watering" stock).

This allowed them to woo reluctant manufacturers into joining a new combination by offering them shares which would bring more in the stock market than the manufacturers had thought their companies were worth. This suspicious situation was brought about by the fact that amalgamating promoters found plenty of stock market investors eager to buy shares in the new businesses, even at prices considerably higher than the per-share net worth of the corporations. The nation's investors believed in the future growth of the new companies and probably expected good dividends and even higher stock prices in the future. In some cases they got what they expected, and in other, less sound cases, they got what they deserved. The success of the investments varied greatly, depending on the particular company. The willingness of investors to pay high prices for stocks made it possible for the promoters and underwriters like Morgan to make enormous profits, and for the owners of previously independent concerns to get more than the real value of their businesses when they joined a combination. The result was that the owners of autonomous businesses found combination increasingly attractive.

During the decade after 1895, the great merger movement flourished, and nothing like it was seen before or since in the history of the nation's economy. Approximately 300 separate firms disappeared into mergers each year during that time. By 1910, many of the nation's most influential big businesses had been created either through vertical or horizontal growth, or through a mixture of the two. Just a partial list of modern industrial giants already born by 1910 included: petroleum companies such as Standard Oil and Texaco; rubber producers such as U.S. Rubber (now Uniroyal) and Goodyear; metals firms including U.S. Steel, Bethlehem Steel, American Smelting and Refining, Jones and Laughlin Steel, Anaconda Copper, Phelps-Dodge, International Nickel, and National Lead; the electrical manufacturers, General Electric and Westinghouse; food processors such as American Sugar, Nabisco, United Fruit, Swift and

Company, and Armour; as well as scores of others including American Tobacco, du Pont, Pittsburg Plate Glass, American Can, Allis-Chalmers, International Harvester, Singer, and Eastman Kodak. It is no exaggeration to say that the structure of the twentieth century American economy had been reshaped by the end of the century's first decade.

In almost every branch of industry, producers tried to create large-scale businesses. Some, like the ones mentioned in the preceding paragraph, were successes. A great many, though, were not, as Arthur Dewing's *Corporate Promotions and Reorganizations* (1914) showed. Many rose like mushrooms in the night and disappeared almost as quickly. Among the giants that might have been but which failed to achieve long-run success, one could list such unfamiliar firms as American Bicycle, National Starch, U.S. Leather, American Glue, National Salt, National Cordage, Standard Rope & Twine, United Button Company, American Wringer, American Grass Twine, National Novelty, Consolidated Cotton Oil, American Woodworking Machinery, U.S. Dyewood and Extract, American Soda Fountain, National Wallpaper, Mt. Vernon-Woodberry Cotton Duck, and many more.

An early and spectacular example of failure was National Cordage. Manufacturers of cordage (rope and twine) tried associations and pools in the 1870s and 1880s which, of course, did not bring the stability and security the producers wanted. In 1887 four of the leading companies took the next step, uniting to form the National Cordage Company. In an attempt to gain control of the industry, the cordage combination embarked on an ambitious program of expansion, acquiring additional mills which gave the company nominal control of about forty percent of the country's rope and twine production by 1890. In the summer of that year, the firm's capital stock was increased tenfold to $15,000,000 and more competitors were brought into the combine. By the early months of 1892, the company effectively controlled approximately ninety percent of the cordage mills in the country. It moved to the forefront of the new industrial giants, it enjoyed the backing of powerful New York bankers, and the financial press hailed it as a sure success.

Within a single year, however, the mighty cordage trust was on the rocks. Competitors sprang up on every hand and the trust's control of the industry slipped badly. Its financial troubles came to a head in the first week of May, 1893—the firm was unable to pay its obligations, its securities plummeted, and it went bankrupt with breathtaking speed. The nation's leading financial journal summed up the events: "Cordage," it announced, "has collapsed like a bursted meteor."

Another notable also-ran in the monopoly sweepstakes was the National Salt Company. That firm arose in the giddying days of the great merger wave as a combination of salt producers in New York state in 1899. By parlaying mergers and imprudent financial agreements with other producers, the promoters of National Salt secured by 1900 control of about eighty-five to ninety percent of the industry east of the Rockies, according to the company's president. The firm then raised the price of salt. For about a year and a half the plan worked well and profits rolled in. The salt trust's fortunes soon suffered a sharp downturn, however, when outsiders rushed into the industry to claim a share of the bonanza. The combine encountered growing difficulty in meeting its financial obligations under the arrangements made earlier to secure its control of the industry. During the course of those troubles, the company defaulted on payments due cooperating salt producers and then tried to escape its obligations by asking the courts to set aside the now troublesome agreements on the grounds that they represented a conspiracy in restraint of trade! The salt barons, it seems, were nothing if not flexible. Their resourcefulness proved unequal to the task, though, and by 1902 the National Salt Company was in receivership.

Although concentration came to almost all industries, it did not "take" in a good many. Obviously, it was not enough merely to have the unscrupulous and greedy outlook attributed to the "robber barons." Riches were not simply lying on the ground for any would-be monopolists to pick up. What factors explained the ability of some big businesses to last while others were quickly cut down?

The work of such scholars as Shaw Livermore, Willard Thorp, G. Warren Nutter, Alfred Chandler, Michael Gort, and others suggests an answer. A look at the history of concentration in modern American industry shows that, in general, the degree of overall concentration and the patterns of concentration have changed relatively little since 1910. The key throughout this century was that big businesses were much more likely to succeed if they were in technologically advanced industries which achieved genuine economies of scale. The difficulty and expense of creating new, competitive firms in such industries as steel, nonferrous metals, petroleum, autos, rubber, machinery, electrical manufactures, and chemicals usually either discouraged most outside competitors from venturing into those areas or explained their lack of success if they did enter. The big companies in such industries had by the early twentieth century a very long lead in terms of capital investment, managerial talent, scientific or technological expertise, and established market positions. Others found it very difficult (though not impossible) to enter and compete successfully with the existing giants. In some industries that involved little in the way of advanced technology, big businesses discouraged competition through heavy advertising and brand names. Makers of cigarettes and breakfast cereals, for example, raised the cost of introducing a new product through massive advertising. Potential competitors were thus discouraged by the very high costs of advertising, and the market share of the existing large firms was protected. Such costs constituted effective barriers to entry into the industry. In most low technology industries, however, it was relatively inexpensive for new companies to enter the market, and correspondingly difficult to maintain a high degree of concentration.

The combines in salt and cordage, for example, were poor gambles from the start. The producers could join together and gain control over prices, but they could not maintain that control. It was too easy for others, tempted by the high prices and profits of the combination, to enter the industry. The supply of raw materials was abundant, the cost of beginning production was low, and no control was possible at the marketing end of the business. When competitors appeared, the combination could buy them out for a time, but eventually it had to succumb to the reestablishment of competition, which broke prices and often resulted in the collapse of the combine. In many industries, then, the workings of market forces insured that society would not be "held up" (at least not for very long) by horizontal combinations. Big business, it was clear, found some industries more fertile soil than others.

Although a few large firms did appear in low technology industries, in general those industries remained relatively unconcentrated. Examples of the latter included textiles, leather, printing and publishing, lumber and wood, furniture, clothing, food, and similar industries. Clearly, the potential empire builder of the turn of the century had to be in the right kind of industry to enjoy the gains secured by the major corporations that endured long after the merger movement. If he was in an appropriate industry, however, he did not find the market constraints on his behavior so strong, and society had real cause for concern about the implications of the advent of large-scale corporations.

The rise of those giant corporations during the years 1860–1910 had produced the modern American economy in which many important industries were highly concentrated. In those industries, the appearance of a few giant companies set new patterns of economic behavior for business. Not only were big businesses impersonal, bureaucratic, capital-intensive, involved in many different functions over large geographic areas, and owned by many persons who did not manage them, but they also competed with one another in ways quite different from the competition among older, smaller businesses. The old days of the kind of competition most economists still talk about—the "Golden Age of Competition," Alfred Eichner called it—were gone forever in many important industries. In their search for stability and order and steady profits, businessmen had eventually created large, integrated, unified firms which, along with a few similar companies, often formed concentrated or oligopolistic industries. These new businesses, unlike the older, smaller ones, very seldom competed by offering prices appreciably lower than those of their major rivals. Price competition, they had learned, could be controlled by businesses so big that their output formed a significant enough share of the market to influence the price behavior of others. In the older economy, the number of producers was so large and the size of each so small that one manufacturer could usually cut his prices without affecting the output and price decisions of the many other firms in the industry. Such behavior under the new conditions of oligopoly and high fixed costs, however, often led to the falling prices businessmen had rebelled against when they traveled down the road to combination. Instead, much of the economy moved into a new era of "administered" prices. Sometimes, as in the case of the steel industry, the largest firm would exercise what came to be called "price leadership." Under that system, the other big producers would simply follow the lead of the major company. Outright price-fixing through collusion was rare, not only because it continued to be illegal, but also because it was not really necessary. The major producers, now armed with improved cost accounting, all knew their costs, and they all had a pretty good idea of their competitors' costs. Therefore it was relatively easy to arrive at a sort of "standard" industry price which everyone tacitly agreed to maintain and which assured a comfortable return on the capital invested in the enterprises.

Instead of competing in price, the oligopolists learned to compete in other, less dangerous, ways. These included different methods of sales promotion (advertising, for example), and different quality or alleged quality in goods and services. The new competition also meant striving for the most efficient internal system of organization and production in order to keep the firm's costs down and profits up. Because the antitrust laws threatened, and because it was much easier and more reliable, big firms seldom tried any more to drive competitors out to secure most or all of the market. Instead, producers settled for a fairly steady share of the market, avoided price competition, and secured the benefits of an economic world much more stable than the one which had produced big business. The new business strategy was to try to maintain a healthy share of the market, but seldom more than half of it, lest the government turn suspicious eyes on the firm. By reorganizing the company and trying to cut production and sales costs to a minimum, profits could be maintained.

Later, businessmen would figure out additional ways to protect or improve their share of the market, such as by introducing concepts of planned obsolescence, the "latest style," and other mechanisms by which the psychological attitudes of consumers could be manipulated or exploited. In some cases, like the automobile industry, the older idea of products as utilitarian objects was replaced by the idea of products as symbols of status, sex appeal, and material achievement. Subtle (and sometimes not so subtle) appeals to pride, prejudice, fear, and the endless varieties of human desire often replaced the older, nineteenth-century appeals to what consumers wanted then (or were thought to want)—thrift, utility, and durability. The new forms of competition were part of a radically different economic and social environment. As Arthur F. Burns correctly noted in his book *The Decline of Competition* (1936), "the rise of the 'heavy industries,' changes in methods of selling, and the widening use of corporate forms of business organization are bringing, if they have not already brought, the era of competitive capitalism to a close." A brave new world of oligopolies, administered prices, non-price competition, and comfortable market shares had replaced the older kind of competition, and many Americans wondered whether the nation was better or worse off.

THREE

The Painful
Acceptance of the
Corporate World

During any period of rapid, widespread upheaval in society, people undergo enormous stress and tension as the old ways yield to the new. Sometimes the resulting shifts in power and opinion even touch off violent, radical reactions. Most often, however, society simply gropes its way to a gradual acceptance of change, and a new brand of social equilibrium emerges, as Robert Wiebe suggested in *The Search for Order, 1877–1920* (1967). The rise of big business and the triumph of industrialism certainly constituted a massive social change during the years from 1860 to 1910, and that change generated much political unrest. Many basic questions were raised about the kind of society Americans wanted, and the economic and social consequences of the new industrial order have continued to be the leading topic of national politics throughout this century.

Uncertainty and unease about the new economic situation took many forms. Protests arose first in the rural areas, especially in the South and the West. The nation's farmers found themselves subject to the fluctuations of a national and often international market for their produce, a complex economic situation they did not understand very well. When their problems began to grow, agrarians tended to blame them on the sinister workings of railroad executives, eastern bankers, industrialists, unscrupulous politicians, and others. Agrarian protest began shortly after the close of the Civil War with the Patrons of Husbandry, better known to history as the Grangers. They soon gave way to agrarian political pressure organizations known as farmers' alliances, whose successes in electing candidates to state and federal offices in the 1880s led them to form a national party in 1892. Joining with dissident workers and with other groups, the farmers spawned the Populist Party, declaring in their famous Omaha platform of 1892 that "a vast conspiracy against mankind" was underway and that a populist crusade would have to be waged to crush it.

During the last three decades of the century, a varied array of protest groups voiced their unhappiness. A small minority of the nation's workers attempted to create viable unions, first in the form of broad-gauged, reform-oriented institutions like the National Labor Union and the Knights of Labor. Those organizations tried to appeal to all segments of working people, and they sought to overturn the wage system and to produce goods through cooperative enterprises. Eventually, such groups merged with the populists in the 1890s. In addition to the farmers and the workers who called for fundamental change, another reform impulse of the period focused on the rather confused fight to alter the currency. A succession of political parties and interest groups from the Greenbackers through the advocates of the increased issue of silver coinage all sought to solve society's problems through inflation. Others emphasized different aspects of the national unease; the followers of Henry George worked for a more nearly equal distribution of wealth through a "single tax" on privately owned land, which they believed to be the key to the exploitation of the people. Many of these reform groups coalesced in the 1890s in the Populist Party and (in 1896) gained control of the national Democratic Party and elected to concentrate their efforts on the silver issue in the famous contest for the presidency between William Jennings Bryan and William McKinley. Bryan's defeat in that election demoralized the agrarian crusade, and that fact, coupled with the return of economic prosperity to the agricultural sector of the economy, resulted in the retreat of farmers from the reform cause. Following the prescription of Kansas populist Mary Elizabeth Lease, they had raised less corn and more hell, until the price of corn rose.

The progressive movement took up the cause, continuing to criticize railroads, giant manufacturing concerns, and influential bankers. The progressives mixed efforts to improve the democratic process (via secret ballots, direct election of Senators, the use of city managers, and so on) with attempts to control or attack businesses, as well as with some reforms which the representatives of big business also favored, such as the Federal Reserve System. Theodore Roosevelt gained a reputation as a "trust buster" by having his Justice Department prosecute several widely hated corporations, and Woodrow Wilson won the White House in 1912, running as an opponent of big businesses.

The reform movements have all been chronicled in great detail by previous historians, and there is little point in recounting the story here. The most comprehensive study of the agrarian movement, John D. Hicks's very sympathetic treatment, *The Populist Revolt* (1931), is still a useful book. Many other studies are available, and the same is true of progressivism; several examples (basically sympathetic but not uncritically so) are Richard Hofstadter's *Age of Reform* (1955), George Mowry's *The Era of Theodore Roosevelt* (1958), and Arthur Link's *Woodrow Wilson and the Progressive Era* (1954). The progressives, like almost all American reformers, have received harsh judgments in New Left interpretations such as Gabriel Kolko's *Triumph of Conservatism* (1963)', which found the movement guilty of being dominated by business. Robert Wiebe's much more sophisticated and balanced treatment of the topic, *Businessmen and Reform* (1962), argued that the business community was divided into hostile factions, some of which took the lead in seeking certain kinds of reform (such as the Federal Reserve System) but shied away from efforts to expand democracy and public welfare services. The progressive era has been the subject of much recent writing, and some of the views advanced by books mentioned here have been criticized and modified. For our purposes, however, we may overlook the details of the historical treatment of the politics and motivation of the reform movements and look instead at some of the basic issues raised by the coming of big business. Some common threads run through the meaning of the political unrest, from the Grangers to Teddy Roosevelt, to Ralph Nader and beyond. We will look at some of the broad sets of issues, considering how the rise of large-scale corporations brought new questions and raised older ones again, and how the nation answered them.

Perhaps the broadest, most diffuse issue that troubled Americans during the fifty years discussed in this book was the fear that the new economic order was destroying America's status as a land of opportunity. Citizens in many walks of life found the revolution in business disturbing and worrisome for that reason. Often persons who enlisted in the fight against big business were those whose jobs had been affected adversely, such as the wholesalers who found giant corporations taking over the merchandising of more and more goods in the changing economy. Small businessmen who were driven into bankruptcy or pressured to sell out to a combination voiced angry resentment. The ranks of progressivism were swelled with people who had belonged to the older economy, but who had little or no place in the world of oligopolies and administered prices. Much of the unhappiness of such people was rooted in their middle-class vision of what America was supposed to be. The ideal of the opportunity for each citizen to acquire and operate his own business died hard. The fascination with the goal of making "each man his own boss" extended throughout much of American society. As big business expanded its dominion over much of the economy, more and more people came to realize that they would probably have to sacrifice the hope of going into business for themselves and accept the idea of going to work for giant corporations.

Many of these basic attitudes were touched upon by critics of big business who testified before the U.S. Industrial Commission, a turn-of-the-century governmental body set up to investigate the problem of growing concentration in industry. Mr. P. E. Dowe, the representative of an association of traveling salesmen (a group hard hit by corporate integration into marketing), voiced the American Dream of the Gilded Age: "Every commercial traveler hopes to attain, both as the goal of the ambitious and progressive businessman and as an equitable return for years of hard work under trying conditions, a business of his own or in conjunction with others." Recalling the traveling men who had been forced to go to work for huge combinations and thus to give up their independence, Dowe noted the passing of the old order and conjured up a bleak vision of the future. "The history of this country," he declared, "gives examples of poor boys who became great men, beginning at splitting rails, tanning hides, driving canal horses, etc., and we all know personally some illustration of self-made men; we have listened to the stories of father and grandsire, telling the younger generation of early struggles, and many instances have been cited where a few hundred or a few thousand dollars started them upon a career to fame and fortune. Trusts have come, however, as a curse for this generation and a barrier to individual enterprise. What will be the prospects for our children? God-Almighty alone knows." This fear of the effects of big business upon individualism and the cherished ability of people to achieve upward mobility lay at the heart of the widespread unease about the emergence of the corporate world. Like the so-called "closing of the frontier" announced in the 1890s by historian Frederick Jackson Turner, the coming of giant corporations seemed to signal the end of an open, promising America and the beginning of a closed, unhappier society. Americans who grew up on the philosophy of Ben Franklin and the dream of the self-made man were troubled by the new vision of success embodied in climbing corporate ladders and moving up organization charts.

A related result of the rise of big business that contemporary and subsequent critics found particularly objectionable was the huge profits made by the men who seemed to threaten the tradition of individual opportunity. Those who created successful large-scale enterprises not only became enormously rich, but they also often lived in ostentatious splendor, flaunting their wealth before a resentful and suspicious population. They built huge, often astoundingly hideous houses in Newport and elsewhere, perhaps as monuments to themselves and their achievements, as Edward Kirkland suggested in *Dream and Thought in the Business Community, 1860–1900* (1956). Some, like Andrew Carnegie, made fortunes every year while many citizens lived in poverty. One's views on this issue, of course, depended on his beliefs about what constituted a fair distribution of income in a society. Several observations should be made about this problem, and the first is that we still know little about the precise patterns of the distribution of wealth and income before the twentieth century. Many historians have recently turned to this problem, and perhaps we will soon know more. Despite the absence of detailed information, however, several broad conclusions seem valid.

First, there has always been, from colonial days on, a very unequal distribution of wealth and income in this country. All the rhetoric about the land of opportunity and the ability of lower class people to achieve higher economic and social status should not obscure the fact that, as New Left tracts such as Gabriel Kolko's *Wealth and Power in America* (1962) remind us, a small minority holds most of the nation's wealth and always has. Recent work by social historians, such as Stephen Thernstrom's *Progress and Poverty* (1964), have also demonstrated how uncommon it was for people from poor families to manage to achieve substantial gains in society. For several reasons, however, that situation did not lead to fundamental political change. Genuine mobility was possible, if unlikely. It took only a few examples of rags-to-riches to convince people that they too might strike it rich. The emergence of big business produced some truly spectacular illustrations of poor boys who became rich, and the popular press ground away at the theme that the application of diligence, hard work, thrift, and intelligence could transform an immigrant telegraph messenger like little Andrew Carnegie into a Steel King. Furthermore, despite the difficulties of achieving upward mobility in the United States, this country offered *relatively* fewer obstacles to mobility than did others. To a nation of immigrants, the contrast with the even greater poverty and economic rigidity in the countries of Europe did make America a land of greater opportunity. As a result, Americans were not perhaps as outraged by the wealth of the "robber barons" as they might have been. The remote possibility that he too might "make it" tended to temper the average citizen's unhappiness about maldistribution of wealth.

Of perhaps more importance, the nation's economic growth during the era of the rise of big business resulted in a general improvement of the situation of most wage-earners. Prices, as was pointed out in the previous chapter, fell very substantially from the end of the Civil War through the mid-1890s. Studies of the behavior of wages show that they fell also, but not as much as prices. By the 1890s, wage levels were roughly equal to or narrowly above their 1870 levels, and wages rose slightly during the decade of the 1890s. Although the data are not as precise as historians would wish, it is clear that most Americans had more material goods in the early years of this century than they had had in earlier decades. In the twentieth century, prices have generally risen, except during the Great Depression, but wages have risen even more. The result, of course, has been the famous American standard of living. The lot of most citizens grew a little better with industrialism and took much of the sting out of the fact that some people's income and wealth increased very much more than others'. The ability of the nation's economy to generate more and more abundance tended to lessen protest about the tremendous concentration of wealth at the top.

A handy political device that could have been used to alter a maldistribution of income, to relieve a "robber baron" of some of his gains if society deemed his material rewards greater than his contributions, lay in the tax structure. A steeply graduated income tax, or a tax on business profits, could have redistributed income. In the political climate of the times, however, that proved impossible. When Congress enacted a very small income tax in the 1890s, the Supreme Court ruled it unconstitutional. Not until the Sixteenth Amendment became part of the Constitution in 1913 was the federal government empowered to tax incomes (though it had done so with ease during the emergency of the Civil War). Even after the income tax was enacted, it had very little impact on the distribution of income, because the tax rates were extremely low for many years. Initially, a tax of one percent was charged on incomes over $3,000, and on incomes in excess of $20,000 a graduated surtax was added, reaching a maximum of only six percent on income above $500,-000.

Americans were not enthusiastic about new taxes even if it was possible thereby to make the Morgans and Carnegies feel the bite more strongly. As a people, we have always tended to identify liberty and property closely, and even less well-off citizens often felt uncomfortable with the idea of taxing the huge profits of big businessmen, if only because that seemed unfair and illegal, even tyrannous. Therefore it proved impossible to alter the nation's wealth and income patterns, though critics like

Henry Demarest Lloyd, Upton Sinclair, and many others kept the issue of excess profits alive. Modern America has continued to have a very uneven distribution of income, but the continued improvement in general living standards has left most people content enough to accept that fact in relative calm. The problem of excess profits and wealth at the top existed before the rise of big business and has endured long after it. A remedy was available to the nation, but no real change occurred because it was not politically feasible—Americans found the remedy perhaps as distasteful as the malady.

Another disturbing aspect of the rise of big business was the ruthless and unscrupulous use of economic power by men like John Rockefeller and James Duke in order to crush their rivals. That is, one thing people found objectionable was the use of certain kinds of unfair competitive behavior, such as secret rebates, selective price wars to drive competitors into bankruptcy and then buy them out at bargain prices, refusal to sell to a wholesaler unless he agreed to market only your products, and similar actions. This kind of problem we will designate as "unfair competitive practices," and it is clear that most Americans agreed then and probably still agree that such economic behavior is unethical, antisocial, and a clear misuse of economic power. Initially, the nation tried to solve this difficulty by passing laws which specifically forbade the use of particular tactics. The railroad regulatory laws, for example, outlawed the use of rebates and differing rates for the same classes of shippers. In manufacturing, the issue of unfair competitive practices involved primarily the problem of discriminatory behavior. A firm large enough to constitute a significant portion of an industry used the power inherent in its size to secure favorable treatment in the purchase of its raw materials, in the transportation of its goods or raw materials, or in the marketing of its products. Often the favorable treatment was economically and socially sound (that is, it often reflected genuine savings in bulk buying, transport, and mass merchandising), but sometimes it was not (as in the case of rebates demanded by big shippers).

Whenever other competitors could not secure equal treatment for equivalent activities, unfair advantages accrued to the large firms.

After a time, however, it became clear that the nation could not outlaw specific practices as fast as inventive businessmen could come up with new ones. As a result, it became the nation's policy to create regulatory agencies with broad general powers to oversee and discipline the competitive behavior of big businesses. Under the administration of Theodore Roosevelt, an agency (the U.S. Bureau of Corporations) was set up to investigate and publicize the unethical competitive methods of offending businesses. It soon became clear that Roosevelt's faith in the effectiveness of mere publicity as an instrument with which to regulate business behavior was seriously in error, and he soon proposed a stronger regulatory body. The eventual answer came in 1914 in the form of the Federal Trade Commission, an agency armed with some enforcement powers, as well as the right to investigate and publicize business activity. As it had done earlier with the railroads, the nation tried to insure socially acceptable behavior by big businesses by creating a regulatory commission to oversee and police the activities of private firms, but not to determine some acceptable degree of concentration in industry. The evolution of the antitrust laws basically came to mean much the same thing. In its 1911 decision in the Standard Oil case, the Supreme Court announced the so-called "rule of reason," which made a distinction between good and bad trusts, though the justices did not use those terms. Giant companies that operated fairly and did not use objectionable methods of competition, the high court indicated, would not be judged guilty of violating the antitrust legislation. The judiciary would not attack any firm on the basis of its size alone, but rather on the basis of its competitive methods.

The main result of those developments was the creation of a new role for government in the economy as watchdog of the private sector, a basically negative, policing role. The combined efforts of the regulatory agencies, the Justice Department, and the courts were supposed to prevent the worst sorts of discriminatory use of economic power. Some critics argue that government regulation has been a failure because business easily dominated the institutions that were supposed to regulate it; others disagree. One's views on the effectiveness of regulation depend heavily on his political leanings and general social outlook, but the new role for government was noteworthy despite arguments over its implementation. The beginnings of regulation did clearly demonstrate that, after the rise of giant corporations, the nation made the political decision that the previously largely private affairs of businesses were subject to public scrutiny, and that the competitive behavior of business was therefore a legitimate concern of government.

The questions posed by the new order in business, however, went beyond ruthless competitive methods. Some critics of big business (including Woodrow Wilson in the 1912 presidential campaign) argued that if only firms could be made to give up their unfair practices, the old system of smaller, more competitive companies would re-emerge. The immoral, underhanded doings of men like Rockefeller, this theory held, had prevented the normal workings of the competitive economy; conspiracy and greed, in this view, explained the rise of large-scale enterprises. Unfortunately for those critics, only a few successful major companies owed their power primarily to the use of such tactics. As we have seen, most of the nation's giant firms arose primarily through vertical growth or through businessmen's ability to purchase or merge with competitors in technologically advanced industries, rather than through the use of unfair competition. In most of the industries where combinations failed to maintain control (the easy-to-enter low technology ones), conspiracy and ruthlessness were inadequate to bring lasting monopoly profits. The perseverence of the successful large businesses, as the evidence about patterns of concentration suggested, was to be explained mostly by their ability to gain economies of scale through costly, technologically complex production or marketing processes. It was surely true that Andrew

Carnegie, John Rockefeller, and other "robber barons" were hard men, unyielding, ruthless, willing to utilize every bit of economic muscle at their command to protect their empires. The economic power they used so coldly, however, was usually based on their ability to produce and market goods or supply services more cheaply than could a much smaller company. Rockefeller's dominion over oil rested ultimately on the fact that, as a result of consolidating production into a handful of giant, highly efficient refineries, his costs were the lowest in the industry. The long-term success of Carnegie Steel was similarly based on greater efficiency, not just greater greed or lesser morality. Society could tell such businessmen to stop using rebates or other forms of arm-twisting, and the result might be to lessen their control or influence somewhat, but definitely not enough to restore the alleged "Golden Age of Competition." Bigness, in short, would not go away once unfair methods of competition were controlled. What then? Was the government to tear down Carnegie's productive mills and Rockefeller's refineries? Were there any reasons to feel that the successful giants could be influenced to use their power in a reasonably responsible and useful fashion?

Though the nation proved unwilling to destroy large-scale enterprises simply because of their size, it could pin some hopes on several factors which worked to limit the dangers posed by giant firms. Most important, although big businesses were resistant to the effects of competition as it was known in earlier decades, they were not completely immune. They remained subject to competition from foreign companies, and some competition could be expected between large firms in different industries. For instance, steel producers might have to compete with aluminum firms in the field of building materials, and both might have to contend in that same arena with makers of other products. Foreign and interindustry competition offered an avenue through which market forces could continue to influence the behavior of large companies. Further, if the corporate giants set prices extremely high and reaped outrageously excessive profits, there was some chance that others would be tempted to enter the industry and compete. Since there were various institutions in the economy that commanded substantial amounts of capital, and since, theorists argue, it was possible for a firm to achieve full economies of scale at much lower production levels than those at which many large corporations operated, new competitors could enter if existing firms presented too tempting a target. Numerous major industries have witnessed the rise of new companies and the eclipse of old ones, though the number of competitors in oligopolistic industries has remained relatively small.

In addition to the continuing role of some market forces, there was also legitimate room for hope that large corporations would at least be as technologically creative as small ones. Critics of big businesses charged that they would grow fat and lazy, that they would not generate the new products or improvements desired by a consumption-oriented society. But, as economist Zvi Griliches pointed out in *The Rate and Direction of Inventive Activity* (1962), "Whatever evidence we have . . . points to no particular relationship between monopoly, oligopoly, or competition and inventive activity. Neither the empirical evidence nor the theoretical discussion has established the presumption of a correlation between the degree of market control and the rate of inventive activity." In that respect, the country was at least no worse off after the coming of big business.

Finally, the nation could hope that the continuing possibility of government intervention would act as a deterrent to extreme abuses of economic power by businessmen. Precedents had been set, and political pressures might revive. It was, therefore, unclear whether the nation was better off with big businesses or without them; the proposition was not an open and shut one, but susceptible to honest and heated disagreements among citizens.

There was a considerable range of such disagreement among Americans, even among those who opposed big business. The succession of reform-minded political movements called for a variety of changes—the Grangers, the Greenbackers, the Knights of Labor, the populists, the single-taxers, the free silver advocates, the progressives, and others all had different prescriptions for a nation stricken with social unrest. Such groups sometimes succeeded in gaining control of state governments, in electing Senators and Congressmen, and even in electing Presidents basically sympathetic to cautious changes. Many of the specific goals sought by the forces opposed to big business were achieved—antitrust laws, regulatory commissions, income taxes, and a host of others. When the reformers had run their course, however, big business remained. It may be argued that large corporations were "disciplined" or "regulated," but it is clear that the political opposition to the corporate giants failed to reduce significantly the extent of concentration in the economy or to break the real power of big business.

There were two basic reasons why the corporate world was accepted in the particular way in which American society acceded to it. First, while it was true that big business threatened important national values, the alternative of destroying it threatened other very significant values. To have forbidden mergers or to have decreed some maximum allowable firm size might have prevented the country from securing the benefits of some economies of scale brought by improved technology, with a possible slowing of economic growth. Such a solution would also have necessitated government intervention in the economy in a way that conflicted with other values. To have accepted bigness and to have sought a solution to the problems of concentrated wealth and power through some variety of socialism, on the other hand, would have required a reversal in national attitudes about that fundamental American institution, private property. Any of these fairly radical alternatives would have called for basic political changes which the populace was simply not willing to make. As a result, some sort of "middle way" was sought.

Second, the rather confused, ill thought-out, and patchwork middle way that was actually selected as an accommodation with the business revolution reflected the very real difficulties involved in assessing the economically and socially optimum arrangement of business units and the problems of implementing that arrangement politically. Even with the improved theoretical understanding of modern economics and the enormously better body of information available about businesses today, no consensus exists about the optimum size of firms in, say, the auto industry. While it is certain that many giant corporations since the rise of big business have been bigger than necessary to derive the maximum benefits of large-scale operations, it is much less clear exactly how big they need to be to secure those benefits. Further, it is not easy to judge what constitutes a fair profit, to prevent the tendency of oligopolists to administer prices, or to know when those prices reflect monopoly power and when they reflect the true costs of production. Even if all the social costs and benefits of big businesses could be identified and measured, the additional practical political and administrative difficulties of engineering the economy were manifold—how could a huge firm be subdivided in a way that was equitable to its owners; how could the several firms created by government order be endowed with a mix of assets that would make them competitive in the long run; how could a repetition of the tendency toward concentration be prevented after a big company was broken up; was competition really increased or decreased when mergers occurred between smaller firms in an oligopolistic industry? Equally important were several still unanswered questions, for example, were there any genuine social benefits in having a larger number of big companies in an industry as opposed to a smaller number of them? (The historical experience of industries like oil and tobacco, in which the government did break up giants into several slightly smaller giants, is not reassuring on this point.)

Any sort of systematic, thoroughgoing government program of organizing and overseeing the structure of industry was, of course, much more difficult to imagine in 1910 than it would be today. Given that fact and the nature of the political system, it was only natural that the nation's political response to the rise of big business was a piecemeal, uncertain, half-hearted answer that left the structure of the economy largely as it was at the close of the great merger wave. Today we are still unable to agree on and implement any comprehensive program of social engineering; it should not surprise us to find that Americans of the progressive era could not do so.

Events in the business world of the last half of the nineteenth century produced a very different kind of society, and they did so with relatively little in the way of social controls. Big businesses arose in the period covered in this book because technological advances and improvements in transportation and communications made them possible for the first time. They spread throughout much of the economy when a few successful examples showed that they were possible, when changes in the legal environment made cartels impossible, when a national capital market arose that was willing and able to underwrite them, and when the political process failed to erect any genuine barriers to their proliferation. As we have seen in this volume, some firms built giant enterprises primarily through the pattern of vertical growth, but most came as a result of horizontal expansion. The creation of the modern economy and the modern corporation did not depend merely on the evil designs and greed of a handful of men. Instead, the most important engine of change was the advancing technology of production and marketing, whose results gave businessmen opportunity and cause to replace the old competitive order with a new, more secure one. Businessmen created the giant corporations because they, more than any previous economic institutions, offered a better means of reducing uncertainty and securing more stable profits. An earlier generation of businessmen would surely have sought those same ends through large firms if conditions in the economy had permitted it. It is in the nature of businessmen to seek profits and to attempt to make those profits as secure and long-lasting as possible. Judgments about whether they do so in ways consistent with the good of society as a whole are basically the collective responsibility of the citizenry through the political process.

By allowing businessmen to create huge corporations and to operate as they have done, we chose to place enormous economic power in the hands of a relatively small group of private citizens. If a majority of Americans do not like the resulting distribution of power and wealth, the quality of life, or any particular or general aspect of the society that flowed from that choice, a range of political remedies are and were at hand.

Although many Americans of the late nineteenth and early twentieth century found the world of big business different and deeply troubling, they accepted it. They created governmental bodies designed to discipline the behavior of big business, and they voiced strong doubts about the impersonality of the emerging corporate world and its implications for their society. But in the end, they accepted it, taking its growing cornucopia of material goods as justification enough. Critics who are quick to condemn that acceptance would do well to ponder the question of historically relevant and feasible alternatives. Men are the product of their historical experience, limited in their choices by who and where they are in history. The rise of big business brought with it all the good and all the bad in the modern American economic system, and it is not easy to see how the nation could have gone down any substantially different road from the one it hesitantly chose. Those who did seek a much more fundamental restructuring of the economy and the society in the wake of the rise of large-scale corporations failed to persuade the voters. If one is to condemn the nation's acceptance of big business, then, as John Braeman has written in a different context, "one's quarrel lies with the values and aspirations of the American people themselves."

Bibliographical Essay

The coming of big business has been discussed by a great many authors from a variety of viewpoints. The works mentioned in this section are only a small sampling, and no doubt some important studies are omitted or overlooked here. For a much more comprehensive listing of relevant additional reading, the student can consult several bibliographies. An early source was A. P. C. Griffin (compiler), *List of Books with References to Periodicals Relating to Trusts* (Washington, 1907). Griffin's work was updated by Francis Cheney's *Cartels, Combines and Trusts: A Selected List of References* (Washington, 1944). A massive and masterly volume is Henrietta M. Larson's *Guide to Business History* (Cambridge, Mass., 1948), the most comprehensive source in the field. Many leading works published since Larson's *Guide* are noted in Robert W. Lovetts's recent *American Economic and Business History: A Guide to Information Sources* (Detroit, 1971).

The background literature on the development of the American economy before 1860 is enormous, but a few of the more important and useful books should be mentioned. A lucid and gracefully written analysis that emphasizes institutional factors is Stuart Bruchey's *The Roots of American Economic Growth, 1607–1861* (New York, 1965). George R. Taylor's *The Transportation Revolution, 1815–1860* (New York, 1951) is a good introduction to the antebellum economy in general, as well as to the development of the nation's transportation network. Douglass C. North, *The Economic Growth of the United States, 1790–1860* (Englewood Cliffs, N.J., 1961), presents an interpretation of national growth based on the cotton trade and the flow of interregional commerce. Albert Fishlow's intriguing book *American Railroads and the Transformation of the Ante-Bellum Economy* (Cambridge, Mass., 1965) is relevant to numerous questions about American economic development prior to the Civil War.

Among recent books which survey the closing decades of the nineteenth century is John A. Garraty's *The New Commonwealth, 1877–1890* (New York, 1968), a good summary of the recent literature. The best interpretive work on the period is Robert Wiebe's brilliant *The Search for Order, 1877–1920* (New York, 1965), which sees the nation looking for different institutions to build a new, pluralistic social order out of the uncertainty which followed industrialization, large-scale immigration, and urbanization. Thomas Cochran and William Miller, *The Age of Enterprise* (New York, 1942) is an early but still useful general treatment of nineteenth-century America from the viewpoint of business developments, tracing the decline of competition and the growing concern with the maldistribution of income. Edward C. Kirkland's *Industry Comes of Age* (New York, 1961) is a thorough chronicle of the era, which also treats the issue of the distribution of the fruits of industrialization. The problem of the reaction to industrialization is discussed in Samuel P. Hays's *The Response to Industrialism, 1885–1914* (Chicago, 1959), one of a number of studies the student might wish to consult.

The first historical "school" dealing with the rise of big business (and one which still dominates many textbooks and classroom lectures) was formed by writers emphasizing the immoral and socially irresponsible role of the "robber barons." Charles Francis Adams, Jr. and his brother Henry set the tone of much later writing in their assessment of the shady shenanigans of early railroad moguls, *Chapters of Erie* (New York, 1886). The brothers Adams blended revulsion with perhaps a pinch of secret admiration, and their lively treatment is still highly readable today. Henry Demarest Lloyd's *Wealth Against Commonwealth* (New York, 1896) was an early assault on the nation's most closely studied corporation, Standard Oil. Lloyd's perspective was that of what might be termed a Christian socialist, and many other historians of this school have shared a similar inclination. A bible for such interpretations was Gustavus Myers' three-volume *History of the Great American Fortunes* (Chicago, 1907–1910), which attacked the methods by which prominent businessmen had acquired their great wealth. After a decline during World War I and the inhospitable 1920s, this critical interpretation was revived during the Great Depression, when Matthew Josephson published what has become the standard work of this school, *The Robber Barons: The Great American Capitalists, 1861–1901* (New York, 1934). In Josephson's view, a handful of businessmen unscrupulously fought their way to control of the entire economy, and (as he argued four years later in *The Politicos*) of the nation's political apparatus as well. Allen Solganick's "The Robber Baron Concept and Its Revisionists," *Science and Society,* XXIX (Summer 1965), 257–269, illustrates the persistence of the robber baron view, and Thomas B. Brewer, ed., *The Robber Barons: Saints or Sinners?* (New York, 1970) indicates the continuing interest in this way of looking at the rise of big business. The robber baron versus industrial statesman framework has spread to other countries as well, as demonstrated by Marianne Debouzy's *Le Capitalisme "Sauvage" aux Etats-Unis, 1860–1900* (Paris, 1972).

An opposing group of historians, generally known as "revisionists," chose to emphasize the positive rather than the negative aspects of the coming of large-scale enterprises. These scholars pointed to the efficiency of big business and its contribution to national economic expansion. This work was usually done in the context of biographies of individual businessmen or firms. Burton J. Hendrick's approving portrait of Andrew Carnegie (*The Life of Andrew Carnegie* [New York, 1932]), for example, continued the tradition of earlier, usually less able books like George Harvey's *Henry Clay Frick, The Man* (New York, 1928). Louis Hacker's *Triumph of American Capitalism* (New York, 1940) admired the drama and dynamism of the unleashing of America's vast economic power; his more recent views were outlined in *The World of Andrew Carnegie* (Philadelphia, 1967). Joseph F. Wall's *Andrew Carnegie* (1971) is a balanced treatment which gives a rich personal portrait of Carnegie the man. Allan Nevins authored a number of volumes with basically sympathetic views of businessmen, including one with a delightfully offbeat title, *Abram S. Hewitt, With Some Account of Peter Cooper* (New York, 1935). Like so many others, Nevins also turned his attention to the oil industry, and he produced *John D. Rockefeller: The Heroic Age of American Enterprise* (New York, 1941). Ralph and Muriel Hidy's carefully researched *Pioneering in Big Business, 1882–1911* (New York, 1955) was another basically positive assessment of the Rockefeller saga. Julius Grodinsky carried the revisionist thrust to its furthest with his laudatory biography of one of the worst sinners in the eyes of Josephson, et al.—*Jay Gould: His Business Ca-*

reer, 1867–1892 (Philadelphia, 1957). In two books sparkling with his marvelous prose, Edward Kirkland assessed the philosophical and psychological dimensions of the era's leading businessmen: *Business in the Gilded Age: The Conservatives' Balance Sheet* (Madison, Wis., 1952) and *Dream and Thought in the Business Community, 1860–1900* (Ithaca, New York, 1956).

Many articles have recounted and assessed the controversy over the robber barons, and they offer a brief guide to the interested student. Hal Bridges, "The Robber Baron Concept in American History," *Business History Review,* XXXIII (Spring 1958), 1–13, surveys the literature and finds the robber baron concept not very useful. Standard Oil rides again in David Chalmers' "From Robber Barons to Industrial Statesmen: Standard Oil and the Business Historians," *American Journal of Economics and Sociology,* XX (October 1960), 47–58. Among many other good articles are Edward Kirkland's "The Robber Barons Revisited," *American Historical Review,* LXVI (October 1960), 68–73, and Thomas C. Cochran's "The Legend of the Robber Barons," *Pennsylvania Magazine of History and Biography,* LXXVI (July 1950), 307–321, which looks at the question in the context of a single businessman, Henry Villard. Fritz Redlich's piece on "The Business Leader as a 'Daimonic' Figure," *American Journal of Economics and Sociology,* XX (January–April, 1953) 163–178, 289–299, points out the dual nature (destructive and creative) of the businessmen of the Gilded Age. In the *Journal of the History of the Behavioral Sciences,* IV (January 1968), 347, Merle Curti and Peter Karsten analyze the varying perspectives of earlier historians of this controversy in their article, "Man and Businessman: Changing Concepts of Human Nature as Reflected in the Writing of American Business History."

From the earliest years of this century, many scholars have ignored explicit moral questioning or defense of the coming of big business and have attempted instead to deal with the era in a more narrowly economic framework. A vast body of amoral studies and sound data was assembled, though no comprehensive generalizations emerged. An early compendium of differing views on concentration was the nineteen-volume *Report of the Industrial Commission* (Washington, 1900–1902), containing testimony given to the U.S. Industrial Commission, a governmental body created to investigate combinations and monopolies. The commission's stance was largely noncommital, but the hearings are a mine of data for students of the period. Information on many early "trusts," including some exotic ones such as the wire-nail trust, appeared in William Z. Ripley, ed., *Trusts, Pools and Corporations* (Boston, 1905). The Ripley volume is especially good on the legal aspects of big businesses. The financial arrangements of the era are explained in Edward S. Meade's old but sound *Trust Finance* (New York, 1903). A group of largely unsuccessful horizontal combinations was considered in Arthur Dewing's *Corporate Promotions and Reorganizations* (Cambridge, Mass., 1914). During the Great Depression, Shaw Livermore examined the industrial sectors in which mergers lasted as well as those in which they soon died out in his article, "The Success of Industrial Mergers," *Quarterly Journal of Economics,* I (November 1935), 68–96. Willard Thorp's 1924 volume, *The Integration of Industrial Operations* (Washington, D.C.), was one of several outstanding contributions he made to the body of data about corporate expansion. More recently, a very good book on the early years of the antitrust laws—Hans B. Thorelli's *The Federal Antitrust Policy* (Baltimore, 1955)— has gathered information on the merger movement. Ralph L. Nelson, *Merger Movements in American Industry, 1895–1956* (Princeton, 1959), measures the pattern of mergers since the great consolidation movement at the turn of the century, while the manufacturing corporations' growing control of marketing during the rise of big business is considered in Glenn Porter and Harold C. Livesay, *Merchants and Manufacturers: Studies in the Changing Structure of Nineteenth-Century Marketing* (Baltimore, 1971). An excellent article which emphasizes the importance of technology in determining patterns of concentration in manufacturing is Alfred D. Chandler, Jr.'s "The Structure of American Industry in the Twentieth Century: A Historical Overview," *Business History Review*, XLIII (Autumn 1969), 255–281.

A number of studies of individual industries should be mentioned. On the railroads, the reader should look at Alfred D. Chandler, Jr., ed., *The Railroads: The Nation's First Big Business* (New York, 1965), which argues that the railroad industry pioneered in managerial, financial, labor, and regulatory patterns which later spread to other big businesses. Thomas C. Cochran's *Railroad Leaders, 1845–1890* (New York, 1953) explores the business mind in that key industry, utilizing the concept of social roles. Robert Fogel's *Railroads and American Economic Growth* (Baltimore, 1964) touched off endless controversies by attacking the established notion that the railroad was "vital" to American economic growth. Fogel argued that a system of canals could have provided an effective answer to the nation's transport needs. Another talented economist who has dealt in part with the time period considered in this book is Peter Temin, whose *Iron and Steel in Nineteenth-Century America* (Cambridge, Mass., 1964) emphasizes technological considerations in the history of that leading industry. Alfred S. Eichner's *The Emergence of Oligopoly: Sugar Refining as a Case Study* (Baltimore, 1969) focuses on the American Sugar Refining Company but advances general propositions about the concentration era, arguing that the enforcement of the antitrust laws converted monopolies into oligopolies. The literature on particular industries is voluminous, and only three articles will be mentioned here. Helen M. Kramer's "Harvesters and High Finance: Formation of the International Harvester Company," *Business History Review*, XXXVIII (Autumn 1964), 284–301, recounts the creation of one large company in an oligopolistic industry. Two especially good analyses of industries are: Richard Zerbe's "The American Sugar Refining Company, 1887–1914: The Story of a Monopoly," *Journal of Law and Economics*, XII (October 1969), 339–376, which provides a somewhat different look at that industry than Alfred Eichner's; and John S. McGee, "Predatory Price Cutting: The Standard Oil (N.J.) Case," *Journal of Law and Economics,* I (October 1958), 137–169, which argues that Rockefeller's company never engaged in selective price cutting to destroy competitors.

The importance of changes in the nation's financial institutions as they relate to the rise of big business is demonstrated in a number of good studies. An outstanding article explaining how the securities of industrial firms came to be available and accepted in the capital markets is Thomas R. Navin and Marian V. Sears, "The Rise of a Market for Industrial Securities, 1887–1902," *Business History Review,* XXXIX (June 1955), 105–138. Vincent Carosso's *Investment Banking in America* (Cambridge, Mass., 1970) is the most thorough treatment of that important kind of banking activity. The power of J. P. Morgan has lured many historians into attempts to explain his role in the coming of big business. A delightfully readable account is Frederick L. Allen's *The Great Pierpont Morgan* (New York, 1949), and the doings of a Morgan partner are described in John Garraty's *Right-Hand Man: The Life of George W. Perkins* (New York, 1960).

During the last ten or fifteen years a new synthesis on the rise of big business has begun to emerge. Its principal author is Alfred D. Chandler, Jr. In a seminal essay published in the Spring 1959 number of the *Business History Review* ("The Beginnings of 'Big Business' in American Industry"), Chandler argued that the coming of big business was a response to the growth of large urban markets which could be reached for the first time after the completion of the national rail network. Expanding his focus to include the twentieth century, he broke new ground with his *Strategy and Structure* (Cambridge, Mass., 1962). He has since altered his views somewhat by emphasizing the role of technology (as in the above article, "The Structure of American Industry in the Twentieth Century"). Abandoning the weary moral concerns of the robber baron historians and their revisionists, Chandler and others have sought to synthesize the data gathered by their "amoral" predecessors. Alfred Eichner's *Emergence of Oligopoly* and Glenn Porter and Harold Livesay's *Merchants and Manufacturers* (both mentioned above) are examples of recent work influenced by Chandler. Louis Galambos's *Competition and Cooperation: The Emergence of a National Trade Association* (Baltimore, 1966) approaches its subject in a similar fashion. By looking at factors such as the technology of production, the nature of distribution, and the kind of markets served by industrial enterprises, and by focusing on the relationships between the function of an organization and its structure, such historians are attempting to understand the rise of big business in more meaningful terms than the concepts of robber barons or industrial statesmen. This work relies more heavily on organization theory and sociology than on economics and owes intellectual debts to Max Weber and Talcott Parsons, as Louis Galambos noted in "The Emerging Organizational Synthesis in Modern American History," *Business History Review,* XLIV (Autumn 1970), 279–290, and as Chandler himself pointed out in "Business History as Institutional History" in George Rogers Taylor and Lucius F. Ellsworth, eds., *Approaches to American Economic History* (Charlottesville, Va., 1971). This way of looking at the evolution of the modern American economy still has much to offer, though there are, of course, many questions it cannot answer.

The broader impact of the rise of big business on American society before World War I still needs much study. We need new data on such topics as income distribution, social and economic mobility, and the relationship between economies of scale and economic growth before the full meaning of the advent of large-scale economic enterprise can be assessed. The recurring question of whether the nation was better or worse off under big business, bureaucracy, and complex technology will continue to depend heavily on subjective beliefs about what constitutes a desirable political and social order. New Left scholars have as yet had relatively little to say about the period covered here, though two books by Gabriel Kolko have drawn much attention,

Railroads and Regulation, 1877–1916 (Princeton, 1965) and *The Triumph of Conservatism* (New York, 1963), in which it is argued that businessmen initiated and controlled government regulation of industry. Judging by the work of New Left historians on the progressive, New Deal, and post-New Deal periods, the Matthew Josephson view will likely be revived in a new and more sophisticated form. Given the central role of big business in modern American civilization, the only sure forecast is that historical interest in the rise of the large-scale industrial enterprise and its meaning for American society is likely to continue.

INDEX